Darling M —
Happy Birthday
1 April 1996 xox P.

GREAT SCOT

GREAT SCOT

The Life of Sean Connery

John Hunter

BLOOMSBURY

First published in Great Britain 1993
Bloomsbury Publishing Limited, 2 Soho Square, London W1V 5DE

PICTURE SOURCES

The James Bond 007 Fan Club Archives, PO Box 007, Addlestone, Surrey:
pages 3, 6, 8 *bottom*, 9, 11 *bottom*
Kenny Edwards: page 4, page 5 *top right*
Kobal Collection: pages 7, 9
Kobal Collection/Eon Productions: page 8 *top*
Sheila McLean: page 2
Scotsman: pages 11 *top*, 12
Val Volante: page 5 *top left & bottom*

A CIP catalogue record for this book
is available from the British Library

ISBN 0 7475 1391 0

Typeset by Parker Typesetting Service, Leicester
Printed by Clays Limited, St Ives plc

To
Mum and Dad

Contents

Acknowledgements

B y the very nature of the task he has set himself, the writer of biographies is heavily reliant upon the memories and co-operation of other people. I am no exception. Many people have been unstinting in their assistance; others have co-operated where asked. All deserve thanks.

First of all, I should like to thank all those who have helped me by replying to my many letters and by speaking to me on the telephone. These include: Richard Lester, Guy Hamilton, Michael Caine, Ian Bannen, Liz Ihre of Eon Productions Ltd., Graham Rye of the James Bond British Fan Club, Billy Garrett of the Royal Scottish Academy of Music and Drama, the American Embassy in London, Eleanor McLaughlin, Herbert Lom, Nicol Mercer, Joyce Snell of BBC Scotland in Glasgow, Brian Baxter of BBC Television in London , Alison Campbell of the Edinburgh International Film Festival, the Australian Embassy in London, the Royal Navy Careers Information Office in Edinburgh, K. R. Merrett and Lyn Laffin of Manchester United Football Club, Donald Cowey of Celtic Football Club, Richard Hunter of the Edinburgh City Archives, Ann O'Connell of the British Tourist Authority, Alain Bourdon of the French Institute in Edinburgh, John Swinney of the Scottish National Party, Jane Daniel of Warner Bros Distributors Ltd., Tony Byrne of BAFTA, the Canadian Broadcasting Corporation, Anglia Television Ltd., the

9

Registry Office on Gibraltar, the Edinburgh International Festival, the Library Centre in Hounslow, Lesley Lind and Robert N. Smart of the University of St Andrews, and others who wish to remain anonymous.

Special thanks are also due to: Brian Donald, boxing correspondent of the Edinburgh *Evening News*, John Cassie, Sheila MacLean, Rab McGinty, Alex Kitson, Val Volante, Max Stewart, Craigie Veitch, Eddie Phillips, John Fee, John Cherrie and Andrew Skirving, Albert Melrose, Mrs Hardy, Gordon Wright, Dorothy Murray, Alvin Rakoff, Frank Hauser, Jim Houston, William McIlvanney, Bill Hawkins, Tom Turnbull, Tom Kean, Dorothy Armstrong and Muriel Robertson, Tom Cox, Donald and Marguerite Lean, Tei Williams of the Oxford Playhouse, Richard Demarco, the staff at the National Library of Scotland and Edinburgh Central Library, Andrew Kirk of the Theatre Museum, the Scottish Film Archive, Edinburgh District Council, Elizabeth Margaret Watson of the Scottish Theatre Archive, Donald C. MacDonald and Dr Norman H. Reid of Heriot-Watt University, the French Embassy in London, Simon Forrest, Bill Brown and Ross Wilson of Scottish Television, Rank Film Distributors Ltd., Doris Gourlay, Kenny Edwards and his wife Mary, Magnus Linklater and the staff of the *Scotsman*, the *Daily Telegraph*, the *Sunday Times*, the *Edinburgh & Lothians Post*, John F. McLennan, Director of the Scottish International Education Trust, the Australian Consolidated Press.

Extra special thanks also to my mother-in-law for help with photocopying, to Louise Allan for letting me use her flat as a quiet haven in time of need, to my mother and father for giving me a childhood and education I probably didn't deserve and, finally, to my wife Diane and my children Sarah, Rachael, Kate and Jack for putting up with all the inconvenience of having a husband and father who must at times have seemed more interested in the subject of this book than in them, and for forgiving me when my mind has been elsewhere.

1

A GRACEFUL ADONIS

1

A Graceful Adonis

*Ragged, snottery nosed and hungry, he had never believed that
was how he should be, and he had found his only available
blueprint for a different kind of life in Hollywood films.*
Laidlaw *William McIlvanney*

Euphamia Connery stepped gingerly out of Edinburgh's
overcrowded Royal Maternity Hospital into the late summer sunshine. Through the thin soles of her pumps she could
feel the warmth of the Laurieston Place pavements, heated all
day by the beating sun. The year was 1930 and it had been one
of the warmest summers in living memory. As she walked
awkwardly across the hot pavement to the waiting taxi, she
carried, nervously and inexpertly, a swaddled bundle that was
the reason for her being in the hospital in the first place. This
was her new baby son Thomas, brought into the world just a
few days previously, on 25 August. He was sleeping now, a
few wisps of jet black hair, like her own, in sharp contrast to
the pale scrubbed skin of his crumpled face. The portents, if
you believed them, were anything but good. The Wall Street
Crash had sent tremors of panic through the financial markets
of the world less than a year previously. The Great Depression
was gaining momentum. Factories were closing. Men were
being laid off. Dole queues were lengthening.

Urban Scotland between the wars was a patchwork quilt of
factories and tenements, all stitched untidily together,
untouched as yet by the nips and tucks of postwar town planning. The dominant form of domestic dwelling in Scottish
towns and cities, for both working and middle classes, was the

tenement flat. Middle-class tenements had been built with style; the large airy rooms had ornate cornices, elaborately panelled casements, carved and ornately tiled fireplaces. They had inside toilets. Some even had a maid's room off the kitchen with a bell to summon the serving girl which was rung remotely by handle in the drawing-room.

Tenements built to house the labouring classes were of a more modest nature. The rooms were smaller and there were fewer of them. A reasonably well-off working family might be brought up in a 'room-and-kitchen', quite literally a kitchen-cum-sitting room with a bed alcove and a bedroom off the main room, and it was to just such a proudly buffed and scrubbed room-and-kitchen that Euphamia Connery – 'Effie' to her friends – was now returning.

It was her 'little palace'. As she stepped cautiously into the taxi and tried to settle comfortably on the seat at the back, she did not think herself disadvantaged. Many were worse off. A less affluent working family might be brought up in a 'single end', a single room with bed alcoves and perhaps a scullery-kitchenette, little more than an institutionalized bedsit.

Toilet facilities for many working-class tenement flats were outside on the stair, shared with other families. Effie's room-and-kitchen was one of these. It had no bathroom and no bath. Tommy would be bathed in a zinc bath in front of the cast-iron kitchen range while she and her husband Joe would occasionally find the time to luxuriate in a trough of piping hot water at the local public baths. Effie had no running water in the flat: cold water had to be fetched from a sink on the landing and heated on the kitchen range. The washing-machine had yet to be invented, and on 'washing day' all the mothers in the neighbourhood would load the family's dirty clothes into the zinc bath, cover the top with a clean sheet and carry it round to the wash-house, the 'steamie', where they would turn a household chore into a weekly social gathering, exchanging news and gossip, afterwards taking the still-damp washing back to be hung on lines behind the tenements to dry.

The taxi ride home was mercifully short. Effie was uncomfortable after the birth of her first-born and she longed to be home in Fountainbridge, a working-class community just a few hundred yards to the west of Edinburgh Castle. It was dominated by the giant Castle Mill, a rubber factory and vulcanizing works owned by the North British Rubber Company.

Today Fountainbridge – colloquially 'Fountainbrig' – is a run-down shabby place, hardly a community at all. It is home, if home's the word, to a school, a telephone exchange, a car dealer, a bingo parlour, a pub, a massage parlour, a sprawling brewery, a few small shops and a scattered remnant of tenements left here and there as first the rubber mill and then the brewery encroached on the surrounding community. It is cut in half by the main thoroughfare, Fountainbridge itself, now, as then, a main thoroughfare westwards out of Edinburgh.

But in the summer of 1930, when Effie Connery was taking baby Thomas home for the very first time, Fountainbridge was a very different place. Those who lived there remember it as a thriving working-class community where everyone knew their neighbours and there was help at hand when you needed it. Kenny Edwards, who lived on the same tenement stair as the Connery family and who was to take the young baby out in his pram in coming years, describes it as 'a hustle-bustle of a place'. Others, just passing through, have a different perception. The tenements, built right on the pavement without the merest vestige of a front garden, were tall and forbidding and blackened with the grime of a hundred factory chimneys. Donald Lean, who was later to attend school with Thomas Connery, remembers it as 'a dark canyon of a place', a place to escape from as quickly as your legs – or the wheels of the motor bus – would carry you.

The name Fountainbridge was adopted in earlier centuries by a family of local landowners to replace the original name of 'Foulbridge', a reference to the bridge over the foul waters of the Dalry Burn, then little more than an open sewer. In terms of smell, the Fountainbridge that Effie Connery was returning to was little better, dominated as it was by the odoriferous rubber mills and the equally odoriferous, if smaller, Fountain Brewery.

As her taxi moved away from the Royal Maternity Hospital and headed down Laurieston Place towards Tollcross and Fountainbridge beyond, Effie could glimpse through the buildings on her left the trees surrounding 'The Meadows', a huge open park behind the hospital in which the children of the southern half of Edinburgh gathered to play football, cricket, tennis, rounders and a dozen other games, all spontaneously organized. Minutes later the taxi rumbled past one of the local schools, Tollcross Primary, a grimly forbidding stone-built Edwardian building erected on the site of the old Fountain-bridge slaughterhouse, at which young Tommy would start his education. Just a few yards past the school was the Palais de Danse, a large dancehall purpose-built in 1920 in the latest Art Deco styles. Right next to the Palais was the doorway into the New Coliseum picture house, then the largest in the city, then Asa Wass's scrapyard (known locally as 'Azzawozzis'), and then Fountainbridge Primary School, which would be closed as a school in the mid-thirties but brought back into use as a centre for the unemployed and, during the war, as a 'civic restaurant', serving dinners to air raid patrol wardens.

Across the road was Port Hamilton, the baronial head-quarters of St Cuthbert's, the local co-operative society, which vied with the rubber mill for the distinction of being the largest employer in the area. A little further along, by the 'Broad Pavement' was MacKays confectionery factory – the 'sweetie works' – beside which was an open site on the corner of Fountainbridge and Gardner's Crescent. At Christmas time this would be occupied by Cadona's Shows, with merry-go-rounds, coconut shies for the children and shooting ranges for the adults. For a couple of months each summer a boxing booth would be erected there by the Stewarts, showpeople who would charge local residents sixpence each for the privilege of standing around the ring and witnessing some of the great fighters of the time such as Boothman Dempster, Freddie Ten-nent from Dundee and Seaman Watson from Newcastle, slug it out over 15 or 20 rounds.

Just seconds after passing these local landmarks, Effie was carefully manoeuvring herself out of the taxi and crossing the road to her home on the top landing of 176 Fountainbridge, directly opposite Tom Foy's public house, Foy's Bar, and just before the giant rubber mill. The entrance to the stone tene-ment was juxtaposed between a gent's outfitters and a baker. Above the door Effie could just make out the words 'McGlas-han's Abdine Works', a remnant of an earlier use of the building. Inside, there were 16 flats, 16 families, four on each level above the ground-floor shops, accessed by a stair which rose from a common passage running through the building from the street at the front to the stair in the middle and then down a few steps – the 'back stair' – and out to the drying green at the back. The back stair was where young couples at the time 'did their courting'.

When Thomas Connery was born, the family lived in a top flat, an attic right underneath the roof with no electricity or running water, only gas, which served for both lighting and cooking. Even the light on the stair was provided by a gas mantle, lit each evening by a lamplighter or 'leerie'. Off the landing outside was a privy which the Connerys shared with their next-door neighbours and on the landing itself was a sink – with cold water only. Cooking was done on the kitchen range, a cast-iron structure built into the fireplace in which the lady of the house each morning lit the fire and which provided both heating and cooking facilities.

When Effie unlocked the door and let herself in, the fire was already lit. Joe, her husband, had set it going before he left for work that morning. Carefully she laid little Tommy down in his 'cot', the drawer from a wardrobe carefully lined with sheets and blankets. At the time, there was nothing unusual about babies sleeping in drawers, at least among the labouring classes of Scotland. He would sleep soundly and safely there until he was big enough for a bed. It would do him no harm. Many were worse off.

Joe Connery was a man who had learned to be fair and considerate despite, or perhaps because of, the privations of a harsh upbringing. He was of Irish extraction, his father a one-time bare-knuckle fighter and a 'street bookie' in the years before off-course betting was legalized. Eventually he passed his 'pitch' on to Joe, but by the time young Tommy was born, Joe was working at the rubber mill just across the road. He had no qualifications and no trade. But what did that matter? The money from the rubber mill was good and, even during the Depression, the job seemed reliable. The factory was so close that he could come home for his mid-day dinner.

To the casual observer, looking back from today's more affluent times, the Connerys may have seemed underprivileged, and the future which stretched out before baby Tommy and his peers in that part of Edinburgh may have appeared to be one of hard work with meagre rewards. But his life was not without its advantages. His parents were loving and he had a good relationship with both of them. 'He had a lovely family,' says Kenny Edwards. 'His mother and father were lovely people. His mother was a beautiful woman and his father was a hard-working man.' In later years Tommy was to have 'Mum and Dad' tattooed on his left arm. His father was in constant employment, first in the rubber mill across the road, then as the mill contracted after the war, as a furniture delivery porter for Binns department store at the West End of Princes Street. His mother worked as a charlady. The lifestyle of the Connery family was little different from that of hundreds of thousands of families in towns and cities throughout Scotland in the 1930s.

While Tommy was still a baby, his family swapped flats with a family who lived on the first floor of the same tenement building. This had a couple of advantages. First there were fewer stairs to climb up and down for access. It also had its own inside toilet. The one disadvantage was that it was at the back of the building, with windows overlooking the *biggie*, a grassy area which had once been four drying greens, the walls between them having long been knocked down. Beyond the *biggie* were the plain brick walls of Simon Henderson's bakery, a sight which Effie Connery grew to detest. She wanted a front flat, and eventually got one on the second floor overlooking Fountainbridge itself. Here she could relax with her elbows on the window ledge, conversing with the neighbours on either side and those passing along the street below. One of her fondest memories of her later years was when, during the war years, she was able to watch the Queen come to open Edinburgh's first 'civic restaurant' in the old Fountainbridge Primary School just opposite.

Even from a comparatively early age, young Tommy would leave the flat and explore the immediate environs, sometimes accompanied by older children like Kenny Edwards, and later on his own. There was little traffic on the streets, and what there was moved at a much slower pace than we know today. There were a few private cars and taxis, there were motor buses, there was the horse-drawn cart of Asa Wass's and the horse-drawn milk floats belonging to the St Cuthbert's Co-operative Society which were stabled at the Fountainbridge end of Grove Street. At its peak, during the war years, the Grove Street stable was home to over 100 horses. Opposite the rubber mill was the brewery and behind the brewery the Union Canal, built to bring coal from the collieries of West-central Scotland to the industrial areas of the east. Running between Fountainbridge and the canal was Freer Street, a self-contained community in its own right, tenements rising high on either side. At the mission hall in Freer Street local children would spend evenings doing gymnasium work, boxing and other games. The area was full of local characters, men like Mr Stewart the boxing promoter, who would stand outside his booth on Friday and Saturday nights trying to persuade aggressive drunks to come inside where they could demonstrate their skills to an appreciative audience. Or old Mr McKay, proprietor of the 'doddle shop' at the bottom of Mill Lane, never seen in public without his bowler hat, and from whom local youngsters would buy a 'ha'pence worth of doddles' (toffees) on their way to school in the mornings.

A few days before his fifth birthday, Thomas Connery started at Tollcross Primary School. This was built to take a maximum of 500 pupils and in those days, with families crowded into tenements in every direction, the school roll seldom fell much below the permitted maximum and class sizes were large. There was also much more movement between schools in an area, and when the roll at Tollcross crept above the maximum, some of the more able pupils would be moved to Bruntsfield Primary, a Victorian red sandstone building in a middle-class area half a mile away which had its own swimming pool in the basement.

The classrooms at Tollcross were big, with high ceilings and large windows set just above the level at which the children would be able to look out. In winter the heating was supplied from a boiler in the basement, but on very cold days a fire would be lit in a hearth in the classroom itself. The playground, like the playgrounds of all Scottish schools at that time, was segregated, girls playing in one half, boys in the other. When the bell rang to signal the end of break time, the girls lined up beside a door at one end of the school building. Young Tommy lined up with the boys beside a door at the other.

Discipline was strict and was meted out with little sympathy. Boys and girls who fell foul of authority received corporal punishment in the form of the strap or *tawse*, a short belt of heavy leather which would be brought down on the palm of the outstretched hand with a sharp smack, enough to jerk tears from the eyes of even the bravest and most determined child, and which left the palm red and stinging for half an hour or more thereafter. Young Tommy's contemporaries at Tollcross remember him as a cheerful but cheeky boy, mischievous rather than bad, who took his punishment bravely, just like the rest.

As a boy, Tommy was not academically inclined. 'I was not enthusiastic enough,' he was to say later, though according to the legend that was to grow up around this child when he reached manhood, he had inherited a natural skill for numbers from his paternal grandfather, the street bookie, and was suspected of cheating at school because he could add up but could not explain how he did it. Despite his lack of interest in school-work, however, he had enough natural ability to warrant moving him, when the time came, up to Bruntsfield Primary.

Among Tommy's friends at Bruntsfield Primary was John Cassie, a lad of the same age who had come over from Ireland with his parents to settle in Edinburgh. Though his father was Scottish, John had Irish blood and when St Patrick's Day came around, he found himself at odds with many of the Scottish boys. 'Being a bit thrawn I use to declare my Irish antecedents,' he says. 'I used to get the heavy end of the stick quite often until Tommy decided that he had an Irish connection as well. He came over on to my side and that meant two of us against the rest. And he was quite a tough wee boy.' Despite his toughness, Tommy is remembered by his schoolfriend as being helpful and obliging rather than aggressive. 'He was able to handle himself, but he wouldn't go looking for trouble.'

At Bruntsfield, as at Tollcross, Tommy had little interest in academic work. 'When Tommy was at school he was carefree about it all,' says John Cassie. 'He didn't seriously apply himself. I remember he hadn't done his homework one time and one of the teachers, Miss Nichol, said: "I don't know what you'll ever make of your life when you leave school."'

In fact, Tommy's main interest lay outside the school walls, on the football fields, the tennis courts and the cricket grounds. He found great enjoyment in physical activities in general, and his evenings and weekends would be spent with other lads from Fountainbridge and Grove Street kicking a tattered ball about on the *biggie*. If they couldn't afford a ball they would make one out of crumpled newspapers tied up with string, kicking it about until it burst. Strictly speaking, football wasn't allowed on the drying greens behind the tenements, and occasionally an irate resident of one of the tenements overlooking would accost a beat policeman on the street in front and send him round to the back with the result that the boys would scatter in every direction.

Whenever they could get hold of a set of pram wheels, Tommy and his friends would build a 'guider', a plank of wood with wheels at either end on which they would pull each other along the road or run at breathtaking, exhilarating speed down the hills of Viewforth or Montpelier Park. If the boys had a little spare cash on a Saturday or a Sunday afternoon, they would hire a canoe or rowing boat at Johnson's Boat Yard on the canal banks and spend half an hour or an hour rowing west towards Polwarth and then back east to do a couple of circuits of the turning basin behind the Palais de Danse and Asa Wass's scrapyard. Even when he did not have the money, young Tommy Connery would go up to the canal to help old Mr Johnson, who owned the yard, with organizing the boats. His intentions were not, however, entirely altruistic. 'Tommy would help out when people brought their boats back in,' says Kenny Edwards, 'and he'd get a free shot.'

When Tommy Connery was a boy, money was tight, yet even in the depths of the Great Depression there was money to be made by an enterprising young lad like him whose other main love was the cinema. One way was to collect empty jam jars and sell them for the few pennies it cost for entrance to the local picture house. Another more or less lucrative sideline involved helping older women to carry their washing home from the wash-house just behind Tollcross Primary School. On other occasions the children would persuade their mothers to get together a bag of rags (or bones) that they could take up the road to Asa Wass's. There, the rags were sorted, woollens in one pile, the rest in another. Woollens commanded a higher price because they could be used as the raw material for 'rag paper' used by artists.

When they had the money, Tommy and his friends would go to the pictures at one of the nearby cinemas, sometimes buying on the way a bag of 'chippit fruit' (bruised fruit) for a penny at the greengrocer. There was an abundant variety of cinemas within walking distance of Fountainbridge. There were the Regal and the Caley on Lothian Road, not to mention the Kings (now the Cameo) further out. There was the Tollcross cinema where the cheap seats were sideways on to the screen. There was the Blue Halls which, despite its unlikely name, was a purpose-built cinema with seating for more than 1,500. There was the Dominion in Morningside, a 'class' picture house, patrons of which had to be suitably dressed: a collar and tie for the men, a smart dress or suit for the ladies. A favourite venue of Thomas Connery's was Poole's Synod Hall on Castle Terrace, nestled below the massive bulk of the Castle Rock. Situated in a building which had once been the headquarters of the United Presbyterian Church, this cinema had a special children's cinema programme on Saturday mornings, and for 'tuppence or thruppence' children were treated to a programme of Flash Gordon, cowboy pictures, adventure films and the like, all of which were meat and drink to young Master Connery.

As they grew older, the boys would stray farther afield, to 'The Meadows' where they would get up scratch teams for football or cricket and play against lads from other areas. At the weekends, on sunny days, they would get on their bikes and cycle out to the fertile pastures of East Lothian on the Forth Estuary – Tranent, Gullane, Dunbar – or to Crammond, a picturesque village on the northern outskirts of Edinburgh where the River Almond flowed into the Forth. Occasionally they would cycle west to the village of Balerno, there to catch fish or swim in the reservoirs.

During the cold snowy winters a totally different vista of outdoor opportunities opened up before them. They would go sledging and snowball fighting on the Bruntsfield Links or ice skating on the duck pond at the bottom of Blackford Hill. At Hallowe'en they would dress up in old clothes and go round in groups 'guising' for nuts, apples and the odd silver coin. As the fifth of November approached, they would expertly erect massive bonfires with self-taught skill on the *biggie* behind the tenements – occasionally on the streets themselves – and patrol them armed with sticks to chase off any would-be wood stealers.

At the age of nine, Tommy took a job as a milk boy at the St Cuthbert's Co-operative Dairy, getting up at five or six in the morning, first to groom the horses at the stables in Grove Street and then to help deliver milk from a cart either around the immediate area or out to Davidson's Mains and Corstorphine on the outskirts of Edinburgh. 'If you got wet you had to sit with your wet clothes on in the school,' Tommy was to recall later. 'You daren't tell the teacher.' By then, young Tommy had a brother, Neil, six years his junior, and the extra cash he brought in from his milk round would help to buy a few little luxuries.

At the time there was nothing unusual about young children working before or after school. Many of Tommy's contemporaries, girls as well as boys, worked for a couple of hours before school to earn pocket money or to augment the family income. Dorothy Murray, a classmate of Tommy Connery's at Tollcross, did even more: 'I remember my younger brother and I used to go out in the morning delivering milk and rolls up three flights of stairs. Then we came back and delivered papers, all before we went to school. At night when we came back from school, we did the evening papers. It was hard going, but it was the norm – nearly everybody did it.'

In many ways, the job was a labour of love for young Tommy. Even before he started at the Dairy, he had spent much of his free time in the Grove Street stable, fascinated by the horses which occupied the stalls there, helping to groom them, to feed them, watching them, talking to them. 'He practically slept in the stables,' says Kenny Edwards.

Alex Kitson, later to achieve national prominence himself as a union leader, was a van driver at St Cuthbert's when Tommy was a boy. Ten years Tommy's senior, he had moved into the Fountainbridge area in the 1930s and had started working for St Cuthbert's when he was fourteen. He had a room in Grove Street over the entrance to the stables. 'Young fellows got to know the vanmen and the vanmen took them into the stables,' he says. 'It was common ground. Tommy was well known because he had a good personality and he was always willing to help.'

When war broke out over Europe in 1939, Tommy's school was evacuated while air raid shelters were built in the play-ground. In the meantime, the children were taught in people's houses, a week here, a week there, a week somewhere else. Though those who lent their houses to this wartime educational effort were happy enough to have young Tommy delivering their milk each morning, some of them were less than enamoured at the idea of having this scruffy urchin from Foun-tainbridge in their houses for lessons. 'You can't really come in here,' they would say. Prior to that young Tommy had been keen on books and reading, but faced with such difficulties he lost interest. At night when the air raid sirens sounded, he and his little brother, Neil, would have to hurry downstairs with their Mum and Dad to the air raid shelter in the backyard where they huddled together listening to the sound of the Luftwaffe bombing the ships in Leith docks. When the all-clear sounded, they would hurry back upstairs to the comfort and warmth of their recess beds.

During the summer holidays Tommy and Neil spent glorious weeks with their maternal grandparents on a farm near Dun-fermline. Shortly after the schools closed for the summer, the boys would catch the train at Haymarket and it would take them north over the Forth Bridge to the Kingdom of Fife where their grandparents would be waiting to take charge of them. The boys immensely enjoyed the time spent on the farm, away from the hustle of life in the Fountainbridge tenements. Here they could roam the hills and fields freely, feeding the animals, guddling for fish in the burn. The holidays finished, they would go back the way they had come, to start back at school again.

In the summer of 1942, just before his 12th birthday, Tommy moved from Bruntsfield to Darroch School. For the most part, those who passed the qualifying exam had the choice of going either to fee-paying Boroughmuir to continue their academic education or to Darroch for an education which was more vocational than academic. Here the boys were taught the ele-ments of technical drawing, woodwork and metalwork, in pre-paration for a life of manual labour; the girls studied sewing, home economics and typing, learning to be housewives, secretaries and clerks. Even at Darroch, Tommy was noted for his lack of application, being voted by the class of 1942 as the boy most unlikely to succeed.

One of the teachers at Darroch, Mrs Hardy, spent her days trying to drum the elements of English, history and geography into an audience which was captive but largely unreceptive to her teaching. She remembers the inattentive young Tommy sitting in the front seat along with a classmate. 'He was a mischievous looking little lad – mischievous eyes and a cheeky wee face. He was mischievous but he wasn't harmful.'

One day during a geography lesson, she was drawing a map on the blackboard when she heard some of the boys tittering behind her back. She turned round and, to her inner shock and consternation, noticed that beside her handbag on the desk were two white mice. Tommy Connery and his friend were trying to get the mice to run round the handbag. 'I loathe mice,' she says; 'I could have run a mile.'

Fully aware that all 40 or so boys in the class expected her to scream in panic and jump on a chair, she steeled herself. 'Oh what lovely little mice,' she said through gritted teeth. 'Can I handle them please?'

It was the last thing on earth she wanted to do, but calling on the last remnant of her courage, she allowed Tommy Connery to lift his mice and put them on her arm where they ran up and down playfully. The whole class started to laugh and Tommy, disappointed that his trick had apparently backfired, turned to his friend and shrugged: 'It's a waste of time. She's no' feart,' he said, meaning that she was not afraid.

Academically, Mrs Hardy found Connery 'very average – not at all brilliant. He wasn't a fool, he wasn't stupid, but just a bare average'. Brighter lights stayed on at Darroch for three years, occasionally graduating to Boroughmuir to finish their education. But like other 'average' pupils, Tommy left Darroch in the summer at the end of his second year, just before his 14th birthday.

Of his classmates at Darroch, many went on to apprenticeships at the naval dockyard at Rosyth on the other side of the Forth, others took apprenticeships in craft jobs – plumbers, joiners, electricians. Having already worked at the St Cuthbert's

Dairy for six years as a milk boy Tommy took a full-time job as a milkman, driving a pony called 'Wee Mary' and delivering milk by the pint to villages on the outskirts of Edinburgh.

Now a handsome and imposing young man, tall and muscular with a shock of thick black hair, he was also known as 'Big Tam' and was earning better money than those of his friends who had taken apprenticeships. He had to start work at half past five in the morning, but he would be finished around eleven – and there was also the chance of overtime, delivering furniture from the St Cuthbert's Port Hamilton showroom further along Fountainbridge. During the war, tall strong young men like Tam Connery were in great demand. 'He would turn his hand to anything,' says Alex Kitson, 'whether it was trying to drive a horse, or trying to carry coal. All these jobs were on the go during the war because of the shortage of manpower.'

On the way back to the Grove Street stable, the young men driving the milk floats would occasionally meet up and challenge each other to a race. It was a common sight in Edinburgh at that time to see two milk floats careering along at breakneck speed, the drivers laughing and calling to each other in friendly rivalry.

One of his fellow milkmen remembers Big Tam with affection: 'After he had finished his milk round about noon he'd rub down Wee Mary, see her fed, then meet up with a couple of friends and go for a pie and a cup of tea and then into the Lothian Billiards Salon up by the Palais. Big Tam was somebody that people looked up to. Even at the age of 14 he had a great personality.'

Just prior to the war, St Cuthbert's had been taking the horse floats off the longer distance milk rounds and replacing them with motorized delivery vehicles. This modernization programme had been brought to an abrupt end with the outbreak of hostilities, when the government commandeered the motorized vehicles for the war effort. The horses were then brought back for the more widespread deliveries, and in areas close to the dairy milk was delivered from hand-barrows pushed by the milkmen. With the ending of hostilities, motorized transport was again introduced for the longer rounds.

Tom Kean had been a delivery driver prior to the war, and when hostilities ended he returned and took over the round with a motor vehicle which Tom Connery had been servicing with his horse and cart. This went as far as the villages of Barnton and Crammond, then in the countryside outside the city. Tom Connery elected to be Tom Kean's assistant – the 'message boy' – with the job of loading the crates on to the van, and then delivering milk to the houses at the other end. He was an enthusiastic worker.

'In the winter in Crammond you could get down to the waterfront with your vehicle but if you got stuck down there you had a terrible job getting back up,' says Tom Kean, remembering how Tom Connery would put a crate of milk on his shoulder, and carry it all the way along the River Almond to the Crammond Brig, doing all the customers in the cottages along the waterfront while Tom Kean himself was able to remain on the main bus route. 'He had no hesitation, and it saved me a tremendous amount of work.'

Nothing, it seemed, was too difficult for Big Tam. Out on the round he would do odd jobs for female customers of all ages. He would fix and carry, break coal and sticks, build fires in the hearth. In return, the two milkmen would be invited in and treated to tea, coffee, even breakfast.

Muriel Robertson, the daughter of one of Big Tam's customers, recollects that he was 'daft' on the cinema. 'His entertainment value was immense as he went to the pictures several nights a week and regaled us the following morning with a detailed enactment of the programme. This was no mere rundown of the story – by no means! – it was all acted out, from end to end of the kitchen.

'We rapidly realized what a tremendous asset we had in our milkman. No need to read the film crits in the *Evening News* any more – just wait till Tommy had done his rounds and we soon worked out where our tastes agreed and where they diverged.

'Tommy must have run one of the slowest milk rounds in Edinburgh. I believe there were at least half a dozen houses where they were regularly plied with light refreshments, not forgetting the horse who would get the odd carrot or bit of apple. How much of the hospitality offered was in the hope of an extra pint is anybody's guess: remember milk was still rationed in those days.'

This is confirmed by Tom Kean: 'In the winter, sometimes

you would get offered tea so much you didn't know where to put it. We had a very good rapport with the customers and Tom was very well liked.'

When the milk round was finished, they would pop into Tom Kean's house on the way back to the stable for a bowl of soup and to put on some dry clothes. Like her husband, Tom Kean's wife had a lot of time for his young assistant. 'She really thought he was a wonderful lad. And I really felt that I had been a very lucky person to end up with such a good lad as Connery.'

By the time he was 15 or so, Tommy had joined the Sea Cadets. This mustered on Tuesday evening every week in the hall on the top floor of his old *alma mater* Bruntsfield School, known for the purpose as *HMS Cochrane*, and was under the overall guidance of a Commander, one Lieutenant Derek Goodbrandt. Here, for the princely sum of 25 shillings (£1.25) a year, Connery would spend the first part of the evening learning seamanship – signals, types of ship and tying knots etc – then, best of all, he would spend the second part in the basement gymnasium, being trained in the art of boxing by ex-Olympic boxer Paddy Fee, at that time one of Scotland's best-known boxing coaches. Big Tam's athletic ability is remembered well by Eddie Phillips, a Sea Cadet contemporary, who was himself later to become a professional boxer. 'He always seemed to excel at everything,' says Phillips. In summer the Sea Cadets would spend a week over in Rosyth aboard *HMS Nelson*, learning seamanship in a more realistic setting. They would swab the decks, play quoits and sleep in hammocks with other Sea Cadets from all over Britain.

As a teenager, Connery's afternoons tended to be spent crouched over the green baize of the snooker table. By all accounts he was a good player, as his father had been before him. Evenings would be spent dancing at the Palais de Danse, with a group of his contemporaries who had given themselves a name – the 'Valdor gang'. The Palais was one of the largest dancehalls in Scotland at the time, with a revolving stage and two resident bands, a big band as the main attraction and a quartet which swung slowly into view when the big band went off for a break. Upstairs, accessed from outside by a separate entrance, a balcony ran all round from which non-dancers, normally older residents of Fountainbridge and surrounding areas, could watch the action while sipping at a cup of tea bought in the restaurant. Often mothers, like Dorothy Murray's, would escort their daughters to the Palais and, while the daughters danced with the local lads, they would watch the dancing with interest from behind the rim of a teacup. 'It wasn't that they were there to spy on you,' says Dorothy Murray. 'It was a night out and they enjoyed it as well. The music was fantastic.'

The Palais, as much a social centre as a dance and music venue, was a magnet for young Fountainbridgers and Edinburgh people from further afield. It was open every night of the week except Sunday – when it ran late-night dances starting on the stroke of midnight – and most afternoons. Local youngsters would go to the Palais at least once each week, many more often. Regular Palais-goers would meet their friends in the same part of the huge dancehall each time they went. Often the men would call on the same partners for the same dances each evening.

Connery's contemporaries remember him as being a 'scruffy' youngster, seemingly uncaring of his appearance. But like them, he would shed his casual clothes, his green tweed jacket and his brown slacks, and don his one dark suit on the nights he went dancing at the Palais.

As dancing and the cinema were the principal forms of after-work entertainment for young men and women at the time, there were many, like Doris Gourlay, one of Connery's regular dancing partners, who went to the Palais every night. 'I went to the dancing straight from my work,' she says. 'I finished at six o'clock, got washed and changed and went right up to the Palais.'

She remembers well the first time she danced with Big Tam, the local milkman. 'He just came up and asked me to dance. You never refused anybody a dance. He was tall and handsome. We got to know each other just by dancing and then he took me to the bus-stop – it was too far to walk me home. He was just an ordinary guy, just like anybody else. But he liked blondes. He was quite funny. I thought he was quite quiet. He didn't have a lot of personality but he was a great dancer.'

Before going to the Palais, the young men in Tam Connery's

crowd would meet at the Lothian Billiards Salon to discuss the day's woes and the possibilities of the night to come over the green baize, the sound of heavy balls clicking in the background. After a few frames the lads would wander out of the smoke-filled halls and stroll along past the New Coliseum picture house to join the crowds clustered around the brightly lit entrance of the Palais de Danse just a few yards further up the road.

'The place was always packed,' says Val Volante, an Italian whose family had emigrated to Scotland and a close friend of Connery when they were both in their twenties. 'Friday and Saturday were absolute mayhem.' Occasionally, pitched battles broke out between groups of youths, often involving American airforcemen stationed on the outskirts of Edinburgh. The Americans, 'overpaid, oversexed and over here' as locals frequently noted, had money to spend and would lavish it on the local girls, much to the consternation of less well-off Fountainbridgers. Jealously led to violence.

Tommy kept himself to himself, more often quelling the trouble than becoming involved in it. He was popular with the local girls on account of his looks, but though he danced with them and occasionally took them to the pictures, he didn't form any long-lasting relationships, apparently preferring male company. To his friends he was affable and easygoing. But to those who did not know him well, his inner shyness and anxiety gave the impression that he was standoffish, reserved. 'He never used to mix much,' says Albert Melrose, a contemporary of Connery's who was brought up in nearby Brandfield Street and who played junior football with him at juvenile league club Oxgangs Rovers. 'He used to keep himself to himself. He was a wee bit standoffish.'

By his 17th birthday, Big Tam had itchy feet. He could see that there was no future in delivering milk around Edinburgh and its suburbs, yet the world was a changing place and surely offered opportunities for someone who was prepared to grasp them with both hands. His evenings at the Sea Cadets had given him a taste for the sailor's life and he desperately wanted to see a little of the world. One day he returned to the room-and-kitchen at 176 Fountainbridge to announce that he had been through to the Royal Navy recruiting office in Bath Street,

Glasgow, and had enlisted for a 'seven-and-five', seven years as a sailor, five in the Naval Reserve. His parents were astonished. He was not yet 18 and was thus not eligible for his two years' National Service. Though the armed forces were a traditional escape route for young Scots lads who cavilled against the restrictions of life in Presbyterian Scotland, Effie and Joe had had no prior warning of their son's plans. But the deed was done and they had to accept it.

A few days later Effie Connery was waving her son off as the train south chugged and clanked out of Waverley Station taking Tam to Portsmouth where, a boy sailor, he would begin his seamanship training and prepare for a life aboard ship. It was the first time Big Tam had been out of Scotland and the Portsmouth barracks were a strange and anonymous place. Discipline was strict and Connery's fiercely independent streak railed against it. It was not quite what he had expected.

In the barracks, *HMS Victory*, he met another Scot, Bob McGinty, who had just returned to Portsmouth from 56 days' foreign service leave. McGinty was 'hanging about' there when he was approached by a tall young man. 'Got a light, Jimmy?' asked Connery. McGinty lit the big man's cigarette and the two fell into conversation, finding to their mutual pleasure that both came from Edinburgh. 'Right away we clicked and we became friends,' says McGinty.

After an initial stint at Portsmouth barracks, the young recruits were shifted to Whale Island, a gunnery school at the northern end of Portsmouth, also known as *HMS Excellent*. Being big and hefty, Tommy was picked for the field gun crew for a competition between Portsmouth, Chatham and Devonport, which involved taking a field gun carriage over an obstacle course.

At lunchtimes at Whale Island, all the classes used to muster on the parade ground and cheer the field gun crews. 'There are two or three gun crews and they all try to do the best times they can,' says McGinty. 'The best crew goes to Olympia to compete against Devonport and Chatham.' Connery's crew won and went.

'He was easy to get on with, funny and humorous, and he could mimic people,' says McGinty. For weekend entertainment the two would board the train to London where they would make for the Hammersmith Palais. 'He was mad on dancing.' At other times they would go to the dancehall in Southsea, a continuation of Portsmouth, at the South Parade Pier.

But already a problem was beginning to manifest itself which would see Connery's naval career cut short. 'He had a bad stomach,' says Bob McGinty, 'but he was terrified to go near the hospital.' Eventually, McGinty was instrumental in persuading him to go to see the doctor. He sent him straight to the naval hospital, known as *HMS Hazler*, in Gosport, just across the water from Portsmouth. 'I used to go and see him and take cigarettes to him. He would be sitting doing rehabilitation, making fireside rugs.'

In the hospital they discovered that this normally strong and healthy young man had peptic ulcers and as a result he was discharged, disabled, from the Navy. His first career move had foundered and he returned, disconsolate, to Edinburgh. Years later he was to tell a journalist that the ulcers had been brought on by his acute anxiety. 'When I was young I was very shy and anxious all the time. I left the Royal Navy with ulcers at 19 – but they started when I was 16. It was just angst.'

On his discharge from the Navy, Connery was given a pension of 6s 8d (just over 33p) per week, rising to 13s 4d (67p). But when they offered him the opportunity to exchange it for a once-and-for-all payment of £90, he accepted with enthusiasm and spent the money on a motor bike.

Thereafter, he entered an unsettled period, drifting from job to job, unable to settle into any one of them. Initially he went back 'on the milk' with Tom Kean, but left after six months or so, having discovered that his discharge 'disabled' from the Royal Navy entitled him to British Legion employment training. He trained as a French polisher and when he finished, went to work for a Mr Starr in Haddington on the East Lothian coast, French-polishing coffins. 'Mr Starr used to go round and visit all the people and mentally measure their length and then order the coffins,' he was later to recall, 'and we could never figure out how he knew the sizes before everybody else. We used to do coffins in mahogany and it was supposed to be oak – so we bleached it. But I suppose whoever was inside wasn't too aware.'

To earn extra cash he worked in the evenings as a 'bouncer' at the Palais de Danse. Here the gentle giant was noted for his ability to pacify without himself being aggressive, to stop fights without becoming involved in them himself. But his heart was not in the French polishing and after a short time he packed it in to take up another job, much less well paid, as a lifeguard at Portobello open-air swimming pool.

During the summer months, Portobello Pool was another popular meeting place for the young people of Edinburgh. They would come from all over the city and beyond to swim, to build up a suntan, to parade their bodies to members of the opposite sex, and to meet friends. The pool was unheated and fed with salt water from the sea. It had been built in the 1930s and was a masterpiece of Art Deco architecture. As a lifeguard, Tam Connery patrolled the edges of the pool making sure that none of the swimmers were indulging in prohibited practices like smoking. Every now and again he had to help keep the pool clean using a net on the end of a long pole to dredge the water for foreign matter. All the while he had to keep a weather eye open for bathers in trouble.

At the pool he made friends with a group of young women who worked the afternoon shift as usherettes at the Regal Cinema in Lothian Road. On warm sunny days the girls would take the bus to the pool in the morning and from there straight to work. Sheila MacLean, a member of the group, found Connery standoffish, and a stickler for the rules. She and her friends nicknamed him 'The Hulk'. 'When I first met Tom Connery I didn't like him,' she says. 'He struck me as being rather clannish.'

Sheila was a cigarette smoker and, like quite a number of others, pursued her habit at the poolside. She remembers Tom Connery running up to her and saying: 'I'm not going to tell you again to put that cigarette out.'

'I used to get annoyed because he didn't check a lot of them and he always checked me,' she says, 'so I took an instant dislike to him.'

Sheila was to get her own back. One day she was working in the cinema and a friend told her that 'The Hulk' had just come in. He bought a 2s 3d ticket (just over 11p) but sat in a seat costing 3s 9d (19p).

'Well, he's done it to me in front of all my friends at the pool,' thought Sheila. 'Now I'll do it to him.'

She walked down the aisle, flashed the torch at Connery and said: 'Excuse me, sir, can I see your ticket.' As a result, Connery had to sit three rows closer to the front.

A few days later Connery got his own back. He came into the auditorium with a 3s 9d (19p) ticket and Sheila MacLean, thinking he had bought his usual 2s 3d ticket, led him down the aisle only to find when she turned to show him into his seat that he was no longer there. He had slipped into the row right at the back.

Later, the two were to become friends and Sheila found out to her surprise that he was a pleasant young man. 'He wasn't a liberty taker. He had a sense of humour, but it was a very very quiet sense of humour. He never got angry much. He never said a great deal. He liked to talk about football.'

At Portobello Pool one of Connery's colleagues was Jimmy Turnbull, a man in his forties with a young family. Turnbull was an enthusiastic and experienced weightlifter and, recognizing in the younger man a natural athleticism and potential for body-building, encouraged him to build his physique. Tam took to the weights with enthusiasm, and began to attend the Dunedin Weightlifting Club, run by Alf Strachan, on Monday, Wednesday and Friday evenings.

The club had started in Milton House Primary School just off the Royal Mile, before moving to an old air raid shelter on 'the Meadows' within ten minutes' walk of Connery's home in Fountainbridge. It was cold, freezing cold, in winter and could be blisteringly hot in the warm days of summer when the group would take the weights outside and perform their exercises, to the interest of passers-by, on the grass. At the Dunedin Connery met, and became one of, a group of young weightlifting enthusiasts. There was Alan Davidson, Pat McLaughlin, his friend Val Volante whose dad owned Ritchie's Restaurant in Cockburn Street, Jimmy Lawrie, a champion weightlifter in his own right, having been East of Scotland champion five years in a row, David Pow, and the brothers George and Tom Ritchie who came up by bus all the way from Prestonpans in East Lothian. The young men took weightlifting seriously, encouraging each other as they trained, exchanging snippets of advice and information. In time, as the club became established, they all went together to Jackson the Tailor's in Leith to be fitted with blazers sporting the club's own colours.

'I can't remember how, but a very happy clique formed,' says Val Volante. 'It was a very tightly knit group of people.' Then, in the fifties, weight training was in its infancy. It was being actively developed in the United States and in the light of more modern techniques which came over from America, the group started to train on Sundays as well.

'Training was so important to us that it became a total lifestyle,' says Volante. 'We trained like madmen. We made sure that we ate the right food, packing in as much red meat as possible, as well as chicken, fruit and eggs galore.'

Diet even extended to the sorts of things the group of weightlifters took to drink. 'We would take a pint of milk and add maybe a half a dozen whole eggs, pour in four or five heaped teaspoonfuls of honey, whip the whole thing up and knock it back. It all contributed to the bulking-up process. Quite simply our ambition was to get as big and as muscular as possible.'

On sunny weekends in the summer the weightlifting group would go down to Gullane, a town in East Lothian with a marvellous sandy beach, where they could show off their muscled physiques at the same time as picking up and improving their suntan. Sunbathing idly on the beach was an ideal rest-day pursuit as it did not involve expending energy – and on rest-days Connery and the others were keen to rest; any physical activity would impede the bulking-up process. On Tuesdays and Thursdays – non-training days – they would go to the Palais. 'But we made sure we didn't dance too much – we didn't want to expend too much energy.'

Though he was an enthusiastic and successful member of the bodybuilding group, Tom Connery could never take the activity quite as seriously as the rest. 'I remember one particular occasion Tom didn't turn up for training,' says Volante. 'It transpired he had decided to go and play tennis.' The rest of the group took a very dim view of Connery's apparent lack of commitment. 'We thought it was terrible, absolutely awful.' But Connery stood his ground. 'Is that all you people can think about?' he asked. 'Has the world come to an end just because I didn't turn up for training?'

For Volante, this was a milestone in his regard for Connery. 'I began to realize then that Tom had a very strong personality indeed – too strong for many people who didn't know him well. Even then he didn't suffer fools gladly. He was a very straight-talking fellow, very penetrating in his assessment of human nature and human character.

'One particular man he described,' says Volante, 'was someone whom he had known for a number of years. In his younger days this man was a fairly sprightly independent man, but after he had been married for a while he changed completely. All the details were picked out and described minutely by Tom. The way he did it showed an understanding of human nature which I thought then was quite unusual.'

Volante also has memories of Tom Connery dissecting the roles of various characters seen on the screens of the local cinemas. 'He wasn't just making small talk and although it wasn't meant to be anything serious, it showed a deep understanding of human character. I remember him probing the layers of meaning in *The Vikings* with Kirk Douglas and Tony Curtis. And another film he talked about in a lot of detail was *The Prisoner of Zenda*. There was a lot of talk about the performance of the "nasty" in it, played by James Mason. Although he was the bad guy, he put in a tremendous performance and that was very carefully analysed.'

Intellect aside, Connery had enough of the narcissist in him to want to show off the physique he was taking such trouble to build. The forum he chose for this was a Mr Universe contest in London. 'The decision was taken maybe about 18 months before this particular Mr Universe contest,' says Volante. 'I remember being a little surprised because although Tom had the height, he didn't have the bulk. I remember him saying that he was going to become like the side of a house. We all thought that he would, but he doesn't appear to have been that physical type.'

While the weightlifting was going on, Tom Connery was still working as a lifeguard at Portobello Pool. Besides irregular hours, the work was poorly paid and his friend Jimmy Turnbull had found a way of supplementing his income by posing, semi-naked, for students at the Edinburgh School of Art. He suggested Big Tam do the same, and for the next year or so Connery, like Turnbull, fitted posing sessions at the Art School around his irregular shifts at the pool – and earned 6s 8d (33p) an hour for his trouble. Much to the amusement of his friends, he had to shave his hairy chest for the budding artists.

Richard Demarco, today a prominent art impresario in Edinburgh, was one of the young art students for whom Big Tam Connery modelled. He already knew Connery from summer days spent swimming and lazing in the sun by Portobello Pool. 'Edinburgh was a much smaller place in the fifties and inevitably if there were personalities you got to know them,' says Demarco. 'I always remember the best-looking man at the pool was this young fellow Tommy Connery and we got to know each other.' As old friends they would spend lunchtimes together at the Art School, sharing sandwiches and views on the disparate lives each of them led.

Demarco started his course at Edinburgh Art School in 1949 and it was when he was in his second year, in 1950, that Connery started modelling. 'It was difficult for the girls to concentrate on doing the life drawing because there was an Adonis in front of them. He had an exotic look about him, as if he belonged to another planet. He was beautiful, but he was also innocent and possessed of a natural grace.'

Connery posed for the students of both evening and day classes. But Demarco apart, he did not make friends with any of the students, even the women. 'Artists' models were lower order,' says Demarco. 'There was a rigid separation between students and models. I couldn't believe that everyone just walked out and left him at the lunchbreak.'

Demarco remembers Connery as being a 'very pleasant' and 'amazingly gentle' person. 'He told me about how unhappy he had been in the Navy, how he wasn't quite sure what he wanted to do. That's why he developed his ulcer. I think he was an individual even then.'

The evening classes were less formal. Thirty or so budding artists, who had each paid 25 shillings (£1.25) for the season, would gather in a studio at the Art School on a Wednesday evening to polish their skills at drawing the human form. Those more interested in life studies stood at the back; those at the front, like Tom Cox, would do portrait work: 'Nobody told us what to do. We just did our own thing. We'd go in and draw for an hour. Then we all stepped out for a ten-minute break, for a smoke and a blether with the crowd round about. On one particular occasion Connery came out with us. We were standing on the balcony comparing what we were being paid. I think the tradesman's rate at the time was something like half a crown an hour.' Cox asked Connery what he got paid for modelling and was astonished when he replied that he was earning several times that amount, not only posing for classes during the day and the evening, but modelling privately for some of the teachers.

Connery's interest in football – in *playing* football – had continued unabated since his schooldays. While playing for Fetlor Athletic, he was spotted by scouts for Bonnyrigg Rose, one of the top junior sides in Scotland, then in dire need of skilful youngsters.

As a result of the interest they showed, he spent a few months playing outside right as a trialist for the club. 'He was a very promising player,' says Andrew Skirving, then on the Committee which ran the club, 'and Bonnyrigg attempted to get him "on paper".' Tam was offered a 'semi-professional' contract which would have earned him ten shillings (50p) a week, and would have entailed turning out each Saturday for fixtures and training a couple of evenings a week. It would have been a big commitment for Connery because Bonnyrigg was a 40-minute bus ride from Edinburgh and that, along with time spent on the field or in the gym, would have taken a large chunk out of his leisure time. Anyway, 'running around on a football field wasn't good for your muscles'. He turned it down.

It was in the autumn of 1952, while Connery was still working at the pool, that he took the step which was to lead to his first job 'treading the boards' of the theatre. An advertisement appeared in the *Evening News* for tall male extras to appear in a touring production of *The Glorious Days*, a celebration of the reign of Queen Victoria, starring Anna Neagle, which would be playing a Christmas season at the Edinburgh Empire. The cast toured with the production – all except the six court ushers who were hired locally in each of the cities at which *The Glorious*

Days was staged. Though Connery had no particular interest in the theatre, he liked the idea of earning some extra cash. He auditioned for the part and for five weeks spent each evening playing the part of a court usher silently watching the old Queen Victoria giving a young soldier the Victoria Cross.

Cash was a problem – as was his job at Portobello Pool. Eventually, unable to stomach the irregular shifts and poor pay any longer, Connery left and took a labouring job in the machine room at the *Evening News*. Here his duties revolved around relatively menial tasks such as keeping the machine room tidy, sweeping the floor and making sure the typesetting machines had adequate supplies of molten lead. It was a job, the hours were regular and the pay was good. As far as intellectual stimulation was concerned, it offered nothing.

'He found it so boring,' says Val Volante, 'that he decided that while he was working he would do everything with his left hand, just to introduce a little bit of novelty and to give himself some kind of challenge.' Volante saw this as an act of rebellion typical of his weightlifting friend. 'He wouldn't accept things the way they were. He had to make a stand.'

In his free time Tom Connery's enthusiasm for weightlifting continued unabated and around the middle of 1952 he and Val Volante caught the night train to London. Connery was to represent Scotland in the 'tall man's' class in that year's Mr Universe contest. Volante – a power lifter rather than a bodybuilder – came along for the ride. Another of the Dunedin Weightlifting Club regulars, Jimmy Lawrie, went too.

Connery and Volante shared a sleeper on the way down to London and Volante, who had had no prior indication of religious fervour from his friend, was astonished when Connery said his prayers before going to bed. 'You can imagine my surprise when, lo and behold, what does he do but get down on his knees and say his prayers. Quite unabashed as well. I was quite struck by this, and quite surprised.'

The Mr Universe contest was not a particularly rewarding experience for Connery or for Jimmy Lawrie. They found that their fellow contestants were much bigger and more prominently muscled. 'We had our eyes opened,' says Volante. 'We were used to our own clique, which I think was fairly civilized and relatively sophisticated. We went down to London and we found these guys who didn't have a brain cell between them. They talked as if body-building was the only thing that mattered. We were absolutely stunned.'

But it was while they were in London for the contest that Jimmy Lawrie saw an advertisement for extras for the stage musical *South Pacific*. This was in the final months of a long and successful run at the Theatre Royal, Drury Lane and was preparing to go on tour. Ostensibly the roles were for 'chorus boys', but these were traditionally of slight build, often openly homosexual, and the chorus parts in *South Pacific* required muscle-men. The roles for this production were, therefore, advertised around the weightlifting and body-building fraternities in London. 'Why not try for a part,' suggested Lawrie. 'What had we to lose?' Connery, who had long harboured an ambition to travel, agreed and they went along to the auditions.

Although Volante did not go along, he heard later about the auditions from Connery. 'They had apparently made it clear that they were looking simply for people for walking-on parts and I think he was amongst a group of people who had had no experience.'

According to Volante, Connery got up on the stage and the casting director, unsure whether he was auditioning for the part of actor, dancer or singer, asked: 'What are you?'

'I'm a bloody man – what do you think I am,' was Connery's typically blunt reply.

'I wasn't mature enough to make a fair assessment of Tom Connery's character at the time,' says Volante, 'but he was very forthright, sometimes to the extent of seeming a little bit cruel. He had a tough uncompromising exterior.'

The auditions were much more successful, at least for Connery, than the Mr Universe contest. He had to invent a background for himself in Scottish repertory theatre, but his luck was in. The casting director was looking for tall athletic men and Connery was offered a part.

'How much will I earn?' he called into the darkness before he left the stage.

'That doesn't concern me,' came the voice of producer Jerry White from the stalls

'Well it concerns *me*,' Connery retorted.

Much later, he was to talk about his break into show business. 'I couldn't dance. I couldn't sing. The producer said it didn't matter. All he wanted was a fellow with a good build who could do handsprings. The wages seemed fabulous – £14 per week when a skilled tradesman at that time was lucky to take home £8. It was an adventure – but there was no future in it for me.'

Lawrie, who was much smaller, did not get a part. They both returned to Edinburgh together, Lawrie to his day job and the Dunedin Club in the evenings, Connery to tell his colleagues at the *Evening News* that his days there were numbered. The revelation was greeted with surprise and scepticism by his colleagues in the machine room. 'He'll be back in Edinburgh before you know it,' they muttered darkly amongst themselves. 'He'll be asking for his old job back.'

2

AN UNEDUCATED SCOTSMAN

2

An Uneducated Scotsman

Most actors are simple, but complicated. Sean is uncomplicated,
but not simple.

Terence Young

As Thomas Connery travelled back to London from Edinburgh to join the cast of *South Pacific*, he had no particular ambitions as an actor. He wanted to earn some money and he wanted to travel. *South Pacific* would, he reckoned, let him fulfil both of those wishes. But it was during those two years spent treading the boards at provincial theatres around Britain that his ambitions formulated and he decided that he could put his early talent for acting out the major roles in films to good use.

His decision was, without doubt, based on finding within himself a real ability to do something which other people could not do. However, it was conditioned by his being taken under the wing of an American actor, writer and director some 25 years his senior, Robert Henderson.

'I had very much an influence over him,' Henderson was later to recall, at the same time refusing to take any credit for 'discovering' his young protégé. 'Sean had it all in him.' What he did not have was any knowledge. These early months on tour with *South Pacific* were not without their problems. Connery was moving in a world of which he had virtually no knowledge and for which he was dangerously poorly equipped. Ice chasms lurked at the end of every sentence and his lack of academic education left him painfully exposed. 'I only became conscious of how uneducated I was when I really got involved in the theatre,' he was to say later. 'It was the realization that those with an education were much more conversant with things. It spilled over into every other field. Anybody who says they didn't have a complex or insecurity at some time because of a lack of education is a liar,' he added. Fortunately for Connery, Henderson was somehow able to discern the real potential lurking within the uneducated Scotsman and began to school him in the art and craft of acting. 'He told me I would have to work at my voice and lose at least part of my accent,' says Connery, and this he tried to do.

As the tour wore on, Connery began to settle into the life of a *South Pacific* muscle-man. He was on stage in the evening, then went back to his digs to play poker long into the night with other men on the cast. If alone, he would write short stories and poetry. On Sundays, the only day off, the cast's football team would arrange games with local teams in whatever town they happened to be in at the time.

In Manchester, Connery shared digs with Henderson, and one night, walking back from a performance, Henderson mentioned the Norwegian dramatist Henrik Ibsen. Connery asked who Ibsen was and Henderson replied by advising him to read Ibsen's plays, works like *Hedda Gabler* and *The Wild Duck*. Connery did as his mentor advised and, when he had finished, asked for more. Henderson made up a list of ten important works which he thought the young man should read, a list including Tolstoy's *War and Peace*, Proust's *Remembrance of Things Past*, Stendhal's *Charterhouse of Parma*, Stanislavsky's *My Life in Art* and Thomas Wolfe's *Look Homeward Angel*. It was not an easy list, by any means, but Connery took it and started visiting the local libraries at the towns and cities which played host to *South Pacific*. He embarked on a vigorous programme of self-education designed to make up for what he had missed academically by leaving school at thirteen.

'When I got into it I realized how much I enjoyed it. It was like a whole new world for me. It was terrific for my ego and confidence to be able to converse, like overcoming a major hurdle. It was only later that I found that the people I admired for being so articulate were ridiculously shallow.'

It was Henderson who discouraged Connery from taking up

professional football with Manchester United when, part-way through the run, the chance arose. Connery was 22 at the time and *South Pacific* was in Manchester for a ten-week run over Christmas. 'The football team drawn from the cast was under the patronage of Matt Busby and afforded the facilities of Old Trafford,' Connery remembers in the Foreword to a book by golfer Bob Torrance. 'There was even talk of my having a trial with Manchester United.' A successful trial would have culminated in a reasonably steady job as a professional footballer and would have paid as much as £25 per week, almost twice what he was earning on tour with *South Pacific*.

'If you're thinking of being a football player, it's a bit late,' said Henderson. 'I think you should seriously consider being an actor.'

'Well, what would I have to do?' asked Connery.

'You'd have to get yourself an education,' was the reply.

Connery agreed, turned the offer down, and went back to his reading list. In many ways this was a remarkable decision. He had been an avid footballer since he was a boy. Acting was a very uncertain business, and a trial for Manchester United, then the largest and most successful football club in England, was the chance of a lifetime.

His decision not only ensured that he could follow a career and, with luck, find a degree of success as an actor, but may also have saved his life. A plane carrying the Manchester United team home from a successful match against Red Star Belgrade in what was then Yugoslavia crashed at its third attempt to take-off from Munich airport and on 6 February 1958 seven of the club's finest young players, the 'Busby Babes', were among the 20-odd people who died in the wreckage. One more, Duncan Edwards, died 16 days later from the injuries he had sustained in the crash.

It must have been at least partly as a result of Henderson's patronage and tutoring that during the two-year run of *South Pacific* Connery moved up through the cast. By March 1954, back at the Kings Theatre in Edinburgh, he had attained a speaking role – saying a couple of lines as the radio operator Sergeant Kenneth Johnston. It is somehow typical of Connery that when asked if the prospect of speaking on stage made him nervous, he replied: 'Oh, no. What for?' He had also changed his name from Thomas to Sean, a name which had probably been suggested to him by the release of George Stevens' classic western *Shane* in 1953. Exit, Big Tam Connery, milkman, bouncer, lifeguard: Enter, Sean Thomas Connery, actor.

According to Val Volante, voracious reading was not the only tool Connery used in his self-education as an actor. 'In any big city that he landed in, he would make a point of going to the courts as often as possible simply to watch how people behaved under conditions of stress. He was interested in people who were in the dock, witnesses giving evidence, a fairly wide spectrum of human characters reacting in different ways according to the level of stress.'

Within 18 months Connery had finished the books on Henderson's list, but he knew that reading alone did not constitute an 'education' for an actor, and nor did studying how people behaved in stressful circumstances. In order to get anywhere he would have to learn the craft, learn it properly. A lack of proper training, he realized, would be a handicap to his career progression. There were two possibilities: enrol for a drama school like the Royal Academy of Dramatic Art (RADA) or find a job in repertory theatre. He chose the latter.

When the tour ended, Connery returned to London. He had a few pounds in the bank, a big ambition to make it as an actor – but no job. While looking for work as an actor, he signed on the dole and resolved to take advantage of any possible way of making a little extra cash. One surprising way he found of doing this was by babysitting when he answered an advertisement placed by Peter Noble, a showbiz writer, and his actress wife, Mary. The Nobles had two young children, Tina and Kara. For Sean, free in the evenings, it was the ideal way of making a little extra cash. As time went by, he became friendly with Peter and Mary and was a frequent visitor at their household, where his path would cross with others in the acting profession.

One such was Shelley Winters, the American film actress who had come to Britain in March 1955 to star in the film *I Am a Camera*. Winters described Connery in her autobiography *Best of Times, Worst of Times* as 'one of the tallest, most charming, most masculine Scotsmen' she was ever to meet. When she arrived at the house, Tina, the Nobles' four-year-old daughter, was sitting on Connery's lap listening avidly to a story he was telling in a very serious voice about leprechauns. 'It was a magical hour and Sean was an enchanting storyteller.'

But storytelling, however enchanting, did not pay the rent and Connery was finding that jobs in acting, the ones he wanted, were a far more difficult matter. He spent a great deal of time trolling around from audition to audition, with only a little success, a couple of walk-on parts on television – as an Italian porter in *The Jack Benny Show*, as a smuggler in the BBC 'Sailor of Fortune' series, as an extra in *The Condemned* directed by innovative Canadian film-maker Alvin Rakoff on the BBC in 1954 and in *Epitaph*, another Rakoff production, in 1956.

Unlike many other directors at the time, Rakoff would intersperse the studio scenes, which went out by live transmission, with location scenes filmed earlier. In some of these, shot at Dover Castle, a gang of brigands was fighting an army. 'We had a lot of fun on it,' says Rakoff. 'For example, in one scene Sean threw a hand-grenade dressed as a pirate-brigand – and then, dressed as a soldier, he received it. When you cut it together, no-one noticed.'

By now Connery was living with his brother Neil in a house near Portobello Road. 'They had the strangest sort of Dickensian flat I'd ever seen or could have imagined,' is how Shelley Winters described it. 'It was only twelve feet square but had three floors piled on top of one another above a shop. And all the storeys were joined by a rickety criss-cross iron staircase that they had painted red. Sean's room was on the top floor. Their three storeys were furnished in a modest but imaginative way, and Sean's room consisted of walls lined with second-hand books and a huge, very thin mattress on the floor with an embroidered quilt thrown on it.'

Though reticent to talk directly about love affairs in her autobiography, Winters did make oblique references: 'In the third-floor kitchen-living room stood an ancient narrow coal stove on which one could cook. It was the only source of heat in the building, but Sean was too thrifty to waste coal when there were sources of heat that he could generate without wasting money. That little house was one of the coldest buildings I've ever been in. But somehow I spent some of my warmest nights there.'

Connery's frugal life style would include a big pot of soup that would last him five or six days. 'It wasn't very good, but it was cheap and plentiful,' he says.

He did manage to get a walk-on part in the Herbert Wilcox film *Lilacs in the Spring* and, later, a very small speaking part in *No Road Back*, a feature-length film adaptation of the play *Madam Tictac* by Falkland L. Cary and Philip Weathers.

Part of the problem for Connery continued to be his inexperience and his thick accent. Casting directors, taken by his brawny good looks, would lose interest when he opened his mouth to speak. He had already sold his motor bike and his poverty became so acute that he even had to sell the rusty boneshaker he used to carry himself from audition to audition. Shelley Winters had to give him money anonymously to pay his rent – he would not have taken cash from a woman. He was later to return this, with interest, by buying her a mink coat.

In a pub in Hammersmith he fell into conversation with a woman photographer, Julie Hamilton, and asked her out. They began to see each other regularly. Julie, tall, blonde, good-looking, was the daughter of Jill Craigie and step-daughter of the then Labour-leader-to-be Michael Foot. Craigie disapproved of her daughter's relationship with the rough-and-ready Scots actor, but by all accounts Connery got on reasonably well with Michael Foot.

It had not been love at first sight. 'My first impression of him was that he was rather large and boring,' Julie was to recall later. 'And those gold teeth and tattoos! They were, to me, the hallmarks of a navvy. I thought: God, what an appalling person!'

But the relationship blossomed – and better times were just around the corner. Robert Henderson, his erstwhile friend and mentor, had by now become involved with the Q Theatre at Kew Bridge, a small theatre which had been set up in 1923 by Jack and Beatie de Leon to encourage new plays and talented young actors and actresses. What it lacked in financial reward it more than made up for in terms of being a 'shop-window' for these young actors and actresses, a breeding ground for young talent to feed the voracious needs of London's West End. Henderson had one of his own plays, *Burning Bright*, performed there and was invited back as a director, initially to direct a stage version of the Agatha Christie novel *Witness for the Prosecution*, which ran for a week from 8 November 1955. He gave his young Scottish protégé a walk-on part in the Agatha Christie play. Even as a non-speaking court usher – and by all accounts a hard-working one – Connery's presence made itself felt. He was dressed for the part in a long black cloak and in one scene had to walk across the stage. As he did so, his graceful carriage made the cloak swirl dramatically. Henderson, realizing that he was unconsciously stealing the scene, had to take the cloak off him.

This break into London theatre was followed, just a fortnight later, by a minor speaking role as Mathias in the Anouilh play *Point of Departure*, directed by Frederick Farley, and the success of his performance in that led, a month later, to a more demanding role in the Dolph Norman play *A Witch in Time*. Top of the bill was Ellen Pollock, playing the witch (or, strictly, the 'Great Great Great Grandmother, who was a witch' as the programme indicated) and she remembers Henderson introducing her to 'an unknown dark chap who he had discovered in the North of Scotland' (*sic*). 'I remember I had to represent a painting that he falls in love with and for the first 20 minutes I had to sit perfectly still (in a mauve light) in a huge gilt frame – so we didn't really have a great romantic scene. But he was a nice unassuming young lad.'

At the Q, Connery was in good company. As Kenneth Barrow observed in his book *On Q*, 'you earned more in rep but at Q you got the chance of working with really good people.' Others who had taken some of their first faltering steps on the boards of the Q included such now-illustrious names as Vivien Leigh, Peggy Ashcroft, Anthony Quayle, Flora Robson, Michael Hordern, Margaret Lockwood, Donald Sinden, Joan Collins and Roger Moore. Unfortunately for Connery, just a few months after he started appearing there, in February 1956, the theatre closed because of lack of funds to provide improvements required under fire safety regulations.

By now the money he had saved during *South Pacific* was long gone and he was struggling to find the rent for his room located in Kilburn. But he had taken on an agent, the young and lively Richard Hatton, and better times were once again just around the corner. This time it was his attractiveness to the opposite sex which came to his rescue.

Rakoff remembers Connery as being 'desperate' for acting work and as a result of the young man's pleading, gave him another two parts in *The Condemned*, one in the studio as a soldier guarding a condemned man, another as a madman banging his tin cup against the prison window bars as the guards walked past. 'Sean was one of these people who used to ring up almost annoyingly and say "Please, haven't you got something I could do this week." One never gave him a speaking part. He was just considered a rather good reasonably intelligent non-speaking actor.'

British playwrights had been slow to adapt to the demands of the new television medium and in order to get suitable material, directors like Rakoff would bring to Britain plays which had already been successful on American television. By the mid-fifties, Rakoff was on good terms with a number of eminent American television writers, including Rod Serling who had just had a play on US television called *Requiem for a Heavyweight*. Rakoff heard about the play in the spring of 1957 and called Serling for a copy of the script. 'My secretary at the time read it first and said I'd like it. She was right.' When he was casting *Requiem*, Rakoff decided to bring over Jack Palance, who had played the lead in the American television production of the play.

Requiem for a Heavyweight is about the fate of a punch-drunk American boxer, 'Mountain' McLintock. McLintock had once been a good boxer, in the running for the world title. By now his body has had enough: he is told another fight might leave him blind, and consequently he has to make way for a younger man. McLintock's faith in his manager is shaken when the latter tries to trade on his reputation by dressing him up in a costume and selling him as a wrestler. In the pivotal scene, the manager tries to persuade him to dress up as a clown in a coonskin cap. McLintock refuses and, fighting the degradation, humiliation and bewilderment with which he is faced, makes the round of the job agencies, eventually finding a job counselling children in an American summer camp. Palance, with his craggy looks and authentic American accent, was ideal for the part.

But it was not to be.

'At the last moment, on the Friday before rehearsals were due to begin, Mr Palance's agent said he wouldn't be appearing for the rehearsal on the Monday.' The American had other commitments and Rakoff would have to find someone else to star in his new television play. 'I spent the rest of the weekend trying to find someone.' He had already cast as the leading lady Jacqueline Hill, whom he was, incidentally, later to marry.

By Saturday afternoon, having auditioned 'a good two dozen' potential 'Mountain' McLintocks, Rakoff was still unsure. He rang Jackie to see if she had any suggestions as to who should play opposite her.

'Have you tried Sean Connery?' she asked.

'Sean?' said Rakoff, bemused. 'What do you mean? He can't speak without that brogue and he mumbles everything.'

'The ladies would like it if you cast him,' came the reply from the other end of the line.

On the basis of Jackie's advice, Rakoff phoned Richard Hatton and invited Sean Connery round for an audition. When Connery arrived he was handed a copy of the script for *Requiem* and given an hour to sit and read it.

'I told him which scenes we were going to do,' says Rakoff, 'told him what the story was about, told him what I expected the character to be like. He came back, asked a few questions and then gave me his verbalization. I was not unimpressed. You can't tell much from a short audition but you can get an inkling of an actor's potential. I said I'd probably recall him the next day.'

By the Sunday, Rakoff had produced a short-list of four potential candidates for the role, one of them Sean Connery. The candidates came back and by Sunday night Rakoff had decided that Connery, the ex-navy boxer with the brawny good looks, would have the part. It was to be Connery's first, and in many ways his most important, screen break.

'Physically he was right for the part. He was a big lad, well over six feet when he stood up. He understood the emotional needs of the character, who was trying to better himself. He understood the need not to be degraded or humiliated no matter what happens. He also had a love of Americanisms and Americana.'

Connery's boxing experience was also useful. The play contained a number of fight scenes opening with 'Mountain' McLintock being knocked out. 'It was choreographed, but it helps if you've actually boxed.'

In the script 'Mountain' McLintock was described as 'a mouthful of teeth, a big smile and curly haired', a description which, says Rakoff, 'pretty well fit' the Sean Connery who had appeared in *The Condemned* and who turned up for audition that weekend – 'except that by the time we get to do *Requiem for a Heavyweight* this man is supposed to be a little bit punchy and a little bit scarred. There was one speech where he asks "Who's going to love me. Look how ugly I am" which didn't quite fit.'

The rehearsals did not go well. Rakoff found that Connery 'needed a lot of help' with the part. Perhaps surprisingly, the accent was not a problem. Connery was playing an American and had to adopt an American accent, but having spent his childhood and youth watching American films, he could manage with relative ease. 'His name was McLintock so he could have a slight Scots burr.' But according to Rakoff, Connery 'was very tight, very unliberated as an actor. Virtually all the other actors asked me to try to loosen him up, to try to get him to relax.' These included such 'unknowns' as Warren Mitchell and Michael Caine who was to become a lifelong friend. Indeed, this may not have been the first time that Connery and Caine met. Stories abound that they had first attended an audition together or that they had met in an agent's waiting-room. Caine himself claims that they met at a party just after Connery had started appearing in *South Pacific*.

Rakoff gave Connery personal tuition. 'I would run through the scenes with Sean, just he and I, in the empty rehearsal room – even the love scenes – to try to get him to relax, to give him American inflexions, to get him to *act*. He was bright enough and he made some very good suggestions, including some romantic suggestions. He wanted to kiss the leading lady at a certain stage and I thought it was a bit sentimental but I let him try it – and he was right. He was very good at give and take in the director-actor relationship. He was not a great natural actor – but he was keen, willing to learn and willing to listen. Sean has *learned* to act extremely well. I have great respect for him as an actor now. I had respect for him as a man then, but he certainly wouldn't have earned much respect as an actor then.'

Rakoff was not the only one concerned then about Connery's limitations as an actor. His boss, 'a wonderful man called Michael Barry', had to approve the play before it went into the studio. The late rehearsal he witnessed, according to Rakoff, was not Connery's best. 'Michael Barry didn't think much of Sean and asked me if I wanted to replace him.' Fortunately for Connery, Rakoff and the world at large did not agree with Barry.

The play, when it went out, was a critical success and even before the reviews had appeared, both actors and director knew it. 'I thought it was wonderful and I knew it was enough to catapult his career,' says Rakoff. According to *The Times*, Connery was 'physically miscast' but played the part 'with a shambling and inarticulate charm'.

In the days following the screening, Rakoff's opinion of Connery's performance was confirmed as offers of work started to come in. Richard Hatton received phone calls not only from a number of independent film production companies but from Rank and Twentieth Century-Fox.

The established film production companies were worried about the inroads television was making into their audience figures and were anxious to sign up this good-looking young actor on a long-term contract. Was he interested? Even as a young man, Connery had been a hard bargainer. He knew that this was his chance to 'make it big' and he was not going to be rushed into any hasty decisions.

Following his minor role in *No Road Back*, he had two more film parts lined up. One was an unbilled performance in *Hell Drivers*, about a trucking company run by an unscrupulous manager more concerned about getting the loads from A to B as quickly as possible than with observing the speed limits and the laws of the land. The other was *Time Lock*, a film about a six-year-old boy accidentally locked in a bank vault at 6pm on Friday which is timed to open again at 9am on the following Monday, by which time the oxygen will have been used up and the youngster will be dead.

To get away from it all, and to give himself a little time to think things over, Connery and Julie got into Julie's car and motored north to Edinburgh, back to Fountainbridge, to see Connery's Mum, his Dad and his old friends. By the time he got back to London, he had made his decision.

He signed a seven-year contract with Twentieth Century-Fox and started a new period of his life and career. At last, he mulled, he seemed to have made it. He had a steady – and in his terms, substantial – income from Fox. He was on the books of one of the largest film production and distribution companies in Hollywood, in the world. His film career was taken care of and he could now fill his spare time as he pleased – reading, going to the movies, and taking parts here and there on television and the stage. He celebrated his new wealth by buying a car, a Fiat 127, and sat back, ready to take whatever nuggets of opportunity the film industry threw his way.

But his time in Edinburgh had not been entirely trouble free. His parents and friends had not taken to Julie and she for her part had been profoundly unimpressed by his habit of disappearing to the pub with the boys without consulting her. On their return to London they lived together briefly in Connery's new flat in Wavel Mews, Kilburn, before splitting up.

While Connery had been on stage at the Q, he had been seen by Greek theatre director Minos Volanakis. Volanakis was at that point working at the Oxford Playhouse with Frank Hauser, then at the start of his own career as a director. This theatre had closed, bankrupt, in the summer of 1956 and was reopened on 1 October 1956 by the Meadow Players, mostly on the strength of £2,000 which Frank Hauser had raised from his friend Richard Burton, who had been a student at Oxford for six months during the war. Having borrowed the money from Burton, Hauser was then able to raise an additional £1,500 from the Arts Council and £600 from a university fund.

When he reopened the Playhouse, Hauser chose not to go down the well-trodden track of showing a mixture of successful West End productions and Thirties comedies, realizing that his potential audiences could already get this diet by travelling up to London.

Instead, he chose what many saw as a potentially fatal programme of serious plays. 'It occurred to me that if you did new plays you would get better actors and actresses. You would also get the London press to come and review it. And if you got good notices in the London press and people came to see it, maybe it would go to London and produce a royalty for the theatre. That's exactly what happened.'

More importantly, the new policy allowed the theatre and the company to be taken more seriously. Though he could not pay 'star' salaries, Hauser was able to offer relatively unknown actors and actresses big parts in new productions. Once the Arts Council had become interested, a wider range of acting talent became available, 'because if you went to Oxford you might end up in the West End.'

In its first season, the new Oxford Playhouse almost went bankrupt again, being saved by a production by Minos Volanakis. This was Aristophanes' *Lysistrata*, which 'just packed the theatre out'. By now, Hauser was reading a lot of Greek plays 'and finding them absolutely fascinating', and during the second season he asked Volanakis to do another Greek revival, *The Bacchae*. Volanakis had seen Connery, liked what he saw and wanted him to play the part of Pentheus, King of Thebes, in *The Bacchae*. Connery would again be in good company. Others who trod the boards at the Oxford Playhouse at around that time include Dirk Bogarde, Leo McKern and Jill Bennett.

'We all met,' says Hauser. 'Sean was waiting to find out if he had got a part in some film. I remember we were a week into rehearsal and he still hadn't heard and I just went round and said "Get in your car and drive up to Oxford or we'll have to replace you."' Connery, on account of his contract with Twentieth Century-Fox, had little choice but to do the film if it was offered to him. Hauser promised Connery that if he did get the film part he would release him from the play, so Connery got into his car, drove up to Oxford and joined the rest of the cast in rehearsals.

'He was a lovely fellow,' says Frank Hauser. 'He was very warm, very friendly, very eager, very interested in things. He wasn't a boozer. He wasn't a womanizer.'

Connery's performance in *The Bacchae* was noted in the press, though the reviewers were generally not particularly impressed with his performance. According to *Theatre World*: 'As Pentheus, Sean Connery showed a present-day figure, lacking regality, but he made a good trance-like exit after Dionysos had established ascendancy.' *Plays and Players* was scarcely more complimentary: 'Sean Connery's Pentheus was too much on the surface and his American inflections were often irritating.' *The Times*, however, indicated that: '. . . if translator and actor convince us that the moment is genuine, as Mr Volanakis and Mr Sean Connery did between them . . .'

His 'magnificently unselfish' performance later in the year at the same theatre as Mat Burke in Eugene O'Neill's *Anna Christie* – with Jill Bennett playing Anna – caught the attention of the reviewer from *Plays and Players*: 'Mr Connery seized happily upon Mat's Irish braggadocio and also illuminated the man's alternating savagery and tenderness with unfailing conviction.'

Frank Hauser has a director's way of assessing Connery's strengths and weaknesses as an actor. 'He was obviously untrained. The voice was all right but it wasn't a particularly good one. He had a thick Scots accent. But you just accepted it as part of the man and the personality.' This was in the mid-to-late fifties when, says Hauser, 'there was a great enthusiasm for regional accents. He fitted in much better than he would have done ten years earlier.

'He had never studied plays – he'd drifted into acting totally by accident. He needed a lot of help literally with what things meant, how you did them, how you approached the part and that sort of thing. But he was an avid learner, a real demon for work. It was almost unsafe to mention a play to him – if he didn't know it he'd go straight out and buy it. He had a great natural grace. He stood very well on stage, he looked very good and he had a very strong stage personality. He was also very funny. We never did a comedy with him, which was a great pity.'

While working with the Meadow Players, Connery trod the boards with an actress who was later to become his first wife, the husky-voiced Diane Cilento. They had originally met over a year previously, when they were both involved in a television production of *Anna Christie* and they had renewed their friendship at a School of Movement run by a Swede, Yat Malmgeren.

Cilento was the 'wild child' daughter of a wealthy and well-known Australian physician who worked for the World Health Organization, Sir Raphael West Cilento. He took Diane with him when he went to work in America and she attended a boarding school there until, at the age of 16, she was expelled for misbehaviour. At the age of 18, having worked in theatre in the States, she came to Britain and enrolled for RADA. After RADA she became involved in repertory theatre and at 22 married the Italian writer André Volpe, with whom she had a daughter, Giovanna. By the age of 27 she was picking up leading roles in West End productions, and in November 1960 she was playing opposite Sean Connery at the Oxford Playhouse in another Volanakis production, Pirandello's *Naked* (in which, according to the *Times* critic, Connery made a 'seriously unforgettable impression'). It was a measure of his commitment to the theatre at the time that he turned down a part in the film of *El Cid* to appear on stage with Cilento. They were soon dating.

'Diane was a highly intelligent and well-read girl – as well as a *remarkably* gifted actress,' says Hauser. 'Frankly, she was very unlike an average English juvenile actress. There was no mincing about her. She was a strong actress. Very sexy and very attractive. She knew the play, which very few people did. Sean agreed to play the Consul. That was the first – and I think the only – time that they ever appeared together on the stage.'

There were plans to feature them together in another play. 'Diane did a play with Leo McKern called *Queen after Death*. Sean was going to be in that but couldn't make it for contractual reasons.'

The backgrounds of Cilento and Connery could hardly have been more different. He, the son of an unskilled factory worker; she, the daughter of a prominent Australian physician. He, who had picked up his acting skills touring with *South Pacific* and working in repertory theatre; she, with the benefit of a full education including five terms at RADA. He, the steady grafter, imbued since childhood with the strict principles of the Protestant work ethic; she, the young rebel, unbowed by the precepts of convention and authority, disrespectful and daring. In court on a drink-driving charge, having refused to give a blood sample when stopped, she was later to say defiantly: 'I have an aversion to people sticking needles into me.' And as one journalist was later to observe, 'she is the only person I have actually seen in public wearing one of those open-worked silver crochet dresses without a petticoat . . . without looking vulgar.'

One thing they did have in common: good looks. Connery, the tall living Adonis of the life classes at Edinburgh School of Art; Cilento, a sultry blonde, with a small, compact and upright figure, later to be described by a (female) journalist as 'an extremely intelligent actress, who tends to be underrated in this country, simply because she looks so marvellous, has an itchingly sexy voice and writes good books.'

In October 1959 Connery was back in Edinburgh. This time he was playing fifth billing at the Kings Theatre in the 'world première' of a touring production of *The Sea Shell*, a play by the American Jess Gregg, sharing the stage for the first time with the veteran Sybil Thorndike.

Advertised in the local press as 'a new comedy', *The Sea Shell* was anything but funny. In fact it was the harrowing tale of a mother (Sybil Thorndike) who was so possessive that she cut her family off from the world outside to the extent that they became reclusive and hermit-like. The son, played by Connery, escaped this fate because he was 'kidnapped' by the father when the latter decided enough was enough and made his escape. The play centres on the return of the long-lost son and his gradual realization that things were not all that they should be, particularly with his young sister Amy (played by Heather Sears). His efforts to show Amy a little of life outside the house culminate in an emotional crisis, and in the end he leaves home again, this time taking Amy with him.

The play received mixed reviews in the Edinburgh papers. The *Evening News* found it 'a strange and morbid piece', though it also remarked on the 'admirable acting of Miss Thorndike, Miss Sears, Mr Connery and the rest'. The *Scotsman* was more fulsome in its praise: 'The whole cast and direction were excellent and the audience most appreciative. This was a "first night" and the . . . atmosphere was apparent in the packed house before the curtain rose.' Connery's entry, the review goes on, with 'an enquiring look in his eyes, was memorable enough and Mr Connery throughout gives a fine performance'.

While he was back in Edinburgh, Sean Connery made a point of looking up his old friends and neighbours – and some of them made a point of looking him up. Kenny Edwards' mother, Belle, went up to the Kings with her daughter-in-law and went backstage to meet him. They found a queue of reporters standing at the door and a woman telling them: 'You won't get in to see Mr Connery – there's a big queue here.'

'He'll see me,' retorted Belle and knocked on the door.

She remembers Connery coming to the door wearing a short blue satin dressing-gown, showing the hirsute chest. 'Oh my God, Belle, what are you doing here?' he said and, with true Fountainbridge hospitality: 'Come away in.'

'Before we sit down, Tam,' said Belle, 'I want you to dress yourself decently.'

At the end of the week when the play had finished, Connery met up with his old friends in Foy's Bar on Fountainbridge and when that closed at 10pm they borrowed glasses from the proprietor and went across the road to continue the party in his parent's house. Big Tam Connery had certainly not forgotten his roots.

By the beginning of the sixties Connery's theatre career had progressed well; he had had a number of major roles and the reviews had been, by and large, favourable. His film career, on the other hand, had signally failed to take off. The contract with Twentieth Century-Fox had not brought him the leading roles he must have expected.

By the time he had signed up with Fox, the studio system which had discovered and nurtured such stars as Gary Cooper and Clark Gable was coming to the end of its useful life. Long-term contracts would soon be a thing of the past and actors – like directors, cameramen, sound recordists and so on – would be employed on a casual basis, selling their skills to the studios as and when they were needed. Instead of nurturing their new talent, carefully planning his career so that he would be the next rising star, Fox lent him out, sending him for auditions for films to be distributed by their competitors – MGM, Paramount, RKO, British Lion.

Initially, Connery went through what he was later to refer to as his 'too' period – he was 'too big', 'too tall', 'too Scottish', 'too something'. He was being paid quite well by Fox for doing relatively little. As time went by he landed parts, but they were relatively small roles in relatively unsuccessful films. One such was *Tarzan's Greatest Adventure*, in which Tarzan pits his bow and arrow against the rifles of a gang of diamond smugglers. *Variety* indicated that 'Sean Connery [is] ... okay ....' Another was *Action of the Tiger*, released in 1957 and directed by one Terence Young, who in five years' time was to be approached by two North Americans who owned the film rights to most of the James Bond spy thrillers written by Ian Fleming. The story of *Action of the Tiger* had some elements of the Bond books. Based on a novel by James Wellard, it was set in the depths of the Cold War, featuring a gang of smugglers headed by 'a dishonest Robin Hood' running contraband across the Iron Curtain between Greece and Albania and a French girl attempting to rescue her brother from political imprisonment. The location filming was done in Spain, and Connery played the part of a sailor called Mike whose main contribution was to make unrequited sexual advances towards the heroine. It was Connery's biggest role so far and during the filming he approached Terence Young with a question.

'Sir,' he asked. 'Am I going to be a success in this?'

'No,' said Young prophetically, 'but keep on swimming and I'll make it up to you.'

One of the offers of work which had resulted from Connery's appearance in *Requiem for a Heavyweight* had been a substantial part in the Paramount picture *Another Time, Another Place* with Lana Turner in the leading role. The film, made at Elstree studios just outside London, was about a BBC war correspondent, Mark Trevor, who has an affair with an American journalist, played by Lana Turner. When Mark is killed, Lana goes to England to console the widow.

At the time Lana was trying to finish a relationship with her gangster-boyfriend Johnny Stompanato, a known associate of Bugsy Segal and Micky Cohen, a potentially violent man who was apparently unable to give Lana freedom to live the kind of life she wanted to lead. In England, she was lonely and miserable and unhappy with the production. 'There were problems with the script,' she remembers in her autobiography *Lana the Lady, the Legend, the Truth*. 'The actors were inexperienced – as I remember, it was one of Sean Connery's first films, and he often missed his marks or forgot his key lights, to the annoyance of the director.' Against her own better judgment, Turner phoned Stompanato in Los Angeles and asked him to join her. He was there the next day, having flown out under the assumed name of John Steele. In London their relationship did not improve and Stompanato's sojourn ended abruptly when, after several stormy days which culminated in a violent outburst by Stompanato, Turner phoned Scotland Yard and had her boyfriend deported.

In Turner's account, Stompanato and Connery never met, but according to her daughter, Cheryl Craine, people on the set were convinced she and Connery were having an affair, and when Stompanato arrived one day at the studio he pulled a gun, whereupon Connery laid him flat with a well-placed punch.

Another Time, Another Place was a film Connery was later to regret having made. 'I'd love to set fire to . . . *Another Time, Another Place*. It was nothing to do with Miss Turner. She was first-class. One's intuitive senses were saying that the director was an idiot.

'They wouldn't allow me to see the rushes and I came in on the last three weeks of the picture for a role that was to be seen at the start, so I was a scrambled egg in it. I'd no influence or authority at the time, so my protests went unheeded. But at least I learned from it.'

On her return to the States, Turner's relationship with Stompanato had deteriorated even further and things came to a head on one fateful evening when Cheryl, then 14, stabbed Stompanato to death in her mother's home with a kitchen knife. Turner's chaotic and violent private life had diminished her appeal with the American public and the film suffered at the box-office as a result. *Kinematograph Weekly* wrote: 'Sean Connery's talents are taxed to the full in the unrewarding role of Mark.' Despite this, the film established Connery as a leading rather than a supporting actor and it led to the offer of a part opposite Janet Munro in the Walt Disney film *Darby O'Gill and the Little People* playing Michael O'Bride, an Irish cook with an eye for the ladies.

Connery flew out to the Walt Disney studios in Hollywood for the 15-week shoot. Initially, he was accommodated in an hotel in downtown Los Angeles. But late one night something happened which made Disney change their accommodation plans. The phone rang in his room and a voice at the other end, claiming to be a friend of the now-dead Johnny Stompanato, advised him to leave town or 'there would be trouble, big trouble'. Connery was thought to have been implicated in Stompanato's murder and the voice on the other end of the line threatened to exact bloody revenge. As a result, Connery moved into a remote hotel where the 'heavies' would be unlikely to find him. From there he called his old flame Shelley Winters, who by now was in the midst of an unhappy marriage to Tony Franciosa. He was going to take her, he told her, to a barbecue being thrown by singer Ella Logan.

In her 'sexiest outfit', Winters drove out to pick him up. 'He was in some strange motel in Burbank, near the Disney studios,' she recalls in her autobiography. 'He had been working on his film non-stop for over a week.' Though she was worried about being seen at a party with another man, Connery's good looks and easy charm won her over. 'I again realized how manly, mature and magnificent he was. His self-deprecating humour and whimsy made me eager to show him Hollywood, Beverly Hills and Los Angeles.' After the barbecue they went for a drive, with Connery at the wheel of her car. 'After a short struggle with my still-married conscience, I didn't ask Sean where we were going . . . we did not come back to Hollywood until Monday morning.'

Connery's performance in *Darby O'Gill and the Little People* caught the eye of the *Variety* critic: 'Comparative newcomer, rugged Sean Connery makes a distinct impression . . . Connery combines toughness, charm and Irish blarney.' Whereas *Films and Filming* spoke of '. . . the excellence of some sequences [which] cannot disguise the distasteful sadism of others.' The film was not a wild success for Disney and, despite the reviews, they never asked him back.

In 1961 he was again to play an Irishman, a hit-man named Damion, this time in a British production, *The Frightened City*. This was followed by a leading role as a dim-witted soldier in the Anglo-Amalgamated production *On the Fiddle*, which was released under the title *Operation SNAFU* in the US. The film was a failure both critically and commercially.

*

If success in the film world seemed elusive to the young Sean Connery as the Swinging Sixties began, television was a different matter. He was well on the way to establishing himself as a serious dramatic actor in this relatively young medium, as a result of a number of powerful appearances in television plays. In November 1959, for example, in Arthur Miller's *The Crucible*, he gave a performance one reviewer thought 'unusually polished and imaginative', one in which Connery 'carried off the acting honours'. This was followed by another passionate performance in Anouilh's *Colombe* and by a performance in *The Pets*, a play based on *The Hiding Place*, a novel by Robert Shaw, the *Times* critic commenting: 'Finely and uninhibitedly played by Mr Max Adrian, Mr Shaw himself and Mr Sean Connery.'

There were also impressive performances as Shakespeare's Hotspur in two parts of the BBC's 'Age of Kings' series, in *Richard II* and *Henry IV*. The *Times* critic wrote: 'The best performances of the evening came from . . . Mr Tom Fleming as a cool canny and rather shifty Henry IV and Mr Sean Connery as a forceful Hotspur.' In the J. B. Synge classic *Riders to the Sea* in September 1960 he was, according to one reviewer, 'beautifully in keeping' with Sybil Thorndike, playing her son.

The culmination of Connery's television career came in the following year, when he played, first, the part of Alexander in Terence Rattigan's *Adventure Story*, a study of the life of Alexander the Great, and then Vronsky in an adaptation of Tolstoy's *Anna Karenina*. Both performances were well reviewed, but his performance in *Adventure Story* drew particularly fulsome praise. According to the *Times* critic: 'Mr Sean Connery, the conqueror in thrall to his own conquests, recognizing but unable to resist the corruptions of power, played with intelligence and well-directed force; he never, even as a reluctant tyrant, completely lost the impetuous charm on which Mr Rattigan insists at the play's opening. Certain inflexions . . . at times made one feel that the part had found the young Olivier it needs.'

3

A HAND-KNITTED BOND

3

A Hand-knitted Bond

*The lean, hard face had a hungry, competitive edge to it. There
was something swift and intent in the way he ran his fingers
along his jaw and in the impatient stroke of the hairbrush to put
back the comma of black hair that fell down an inch above his
right eyebrow.*

Moonraker, *Ian Fleming*

As he wedged his large frame into the driving seat of his Fiat
127 to set off through the London traffic to the offices of
Eon Productions Ltd., Sean Connery knew that the James Bond
role for which he had been asked to put himself forward had
the potential to take him far beyond anything he had ever done
before. His contract with Twentieth Century-Fox, entered into
some five years previously with such care and consideration
following the success of his performance in *Requiem for a Heavyweight*, had been disappointing and it had only two years to go.
Yes, he had been successful on stage and television, but he had
set his long-term sights on the large screen and though Fox had
'lent' him out to other companies and he had played one or two
fairly substantial roles, he was still, at the age of 31, a relative
'unknown' in the world of films.

The Bond novels had been building in popularity since the
first one, *Casino Royale*, was published in 1953. The fantastic
adventures of a British super-spy locked in close combat with
his Iron Curtain adversaries had first been committed to paper
in January 1952. Ian Fleming, then a journalist on the *Daily
Express*, had sat down to type out the first instalment of what
was to become a long-running annual series of James Bond

novels while on his annual two-month vacation at Goldeneye, his house at Ocho Rios on the north coast of Jamaica. Drafted without a plan, *Casino Royale* took Fleming only eight weeks from the time he started to type out the first page to having the final draft finished. He was later to claim that he had written it to take his mind off 'the shock of getting married at the age of 43', but he had actually finished the first draft of the novel a fortnight before his wedding.

Casino Royale was published in the UK on 13 April 1953 and in the United States on 23 March 1954 (under the strangely insipid title *Too Hot to Handle*) by which time the second book, *Live and Let Die* was about to be published in the UK and the third book, *Moonraker*, had already been drafted.

To the more sophisticated reader of the nineties, conditioned by the novels of John Le Carré and Len Deighton, the Bond books may seem more like boys' adventure stories laced with sex and sadism (not to mention racism and blatant sexism) than serious spy thrillers. They have also been outdated by the ending of the Cold War and the drawing back of the Iron Curtain. But in the fifties and sixties, they were popular throughout the social spectrum, with all ages and both genders, and were immensely successful.

Fleming's background, like that of the novel's hero James Bond, was in the landed gentry. He had been to Eton and to Sandhurst, and one of his aims in writing the Bond novels was to earn enough money to retire in comfortable affluence to Jamaica. The lifestyle of the James Bond character, as glimpsed in *Dr No*, was in many ways modelled on Ian Fleming's own:

> For the rest of the year he had the duties of an easygoing senior civil servant, elastic office hours from around ten to six . . . evenings spent playing cards in the company of a few close friends, or at Crockford's; or making love, with rather cold passion, to one of three similarly disposed married women, weekends playing golf for high stakes at one of the clubs near London.

By the late 1950s a huge James Bond industry was in its infancy. One or two of the books had already been serialized in the *Daily Express*. A Bond strip cartoon had appeared in the same paper. Although the books themselves had been slow to take off in the States, American producers had been quick to recognize their screen potential. Already Fleming had received $1,000 from the American television network CBS for the rights to *Casino Royale*, which had been screened on American television on 1 October 1954 by CBS as part of their 'Climax Mystery Theatre' series with American actor Barry Nelson in the leading role. Film rights for the same novel had been snapped up by producer Gregory Ratoff who was later (much later) to make a film of it for Twentieth Century-Fox. Screen rights for *Moonraker* had been optioned by Rank.

In the autumn of 1958 Fleming was introduced to Kevin McClory by his friend Ivar Bryce. McClory was an Irish film-maker who was at that time making *The Boy and the Bridge*, a film which was to become the official British entry to the 1959 Venice Film Festival. They began to plan a joint production (backed by Ivar Bryce's film production company, Xanadu) provisionally titled *James Bond, Secret Agent*. For the leading role, Fleming favoured David Niven, an actor with whom he had struck up a friendship after meeting him in his club, Boodles. Niven is actually mentioned by name in *You Only Live Twice* when Bond's latest girl, the Japanese ex-Hollywood starlet Kissy Suzuki, is talking about her pet cormorant David. 'I named him after the only man I liked in Hollywood, an Englishman as it happens. He was called David Niven. He is a famous actor and producer.' But Niven was over 50 by the time the first Bond film was being made, and too old for the part. McClory was not happy with any of the existing Bond plots and so he devised a plot himself – including large sequences of one of his own pet interests, underwater swimming – which Fleming then started developing into a film script.

When *The Boy and the Bridge* was released in 1959, it received a cool reception from the critics and looked certain to be a financial failure. According to one reviewer who witnessed its showing at Venice 'it drew only perfunctory applause from an audience which clearly expected something better'. Fleming and Bryce began to lose faith in McClory and approached Hitchcock to direct the film, only to be met with a flat refusal.

By now Fleming was becoming disillusioned with the world of showbusiness and passed his involvement in the script over to the screenwriter Jack Whittingham. While Whittingham was completing the script, Fleming returned to Goldeneye to lick his wounds and write a book based on the ideas he and McClory had thrashed out. Subsequently, he and Bryce decided against producing the Bond films themselves and instead to sell the script to a major production company.

In 1959 Fleming had bought back the screen rights for *Moonraker* from Rank, which had done nothing about making a film of the book. In 1960 he optioned the screen rights for all of the existing novels – apart from *Casino Royale* which was already in the hands of Gregory Ratoff – to Harry Saltzman, a tough and uncompromising Canadian film producer now based in London.

Saltzman had set up with John Osborne and Tony Richardson the successful art film production company Woodfall, which had already produced *Look Back in Anger*, *The Entertainer* and *Saturday Night and Sunday Morning*. Having taken up the Bond options, however, Saltzman was having trouble finding finance for the first film, *Dr No*, until he was introduced to another London-based American, Albert 'Cubby' Broccoli of Warwick Films, makers of *The Trials of Oscar Wilde*. Broccoli, a streetwise cigar-smoking New Yorker, had impressive contacts in the film production world. And he was enthusiastic about the books: 'Fleming's stories were made to be turned into films,' he said.

By now, following the demise of the studio system, films were being made by small independent production companies but were being financed by the 'studios' or distributors. The production company would approach the distributor with a 'package' – the idea, the director, the leading actors, a draft script – and the distributor, if it liked what it saw, would provide the money to finance the making of the film. The distributor would then retain all revenues from the film until it reached break even after which all income would be shared between the production company and the distributor. United Artists came up with a budget of just under $1 million – not a huge amount considering the kind of film they were planning to make and the fact that they were shooting it in colour. Saltzman and Broccoli bought an off-the-shelf company, Eon Productions Ltd., and started looking for a star.

A string of names were being bandied about the London acting profession at the time. Roger Moore's was one. Though the son of a police sergeant, Moore was RADA trained, and could at will adopt the sort of upper-class English accent with which Fleming's Bond would have spoken. He was in his thirties at the time and had been working in Hollywood since 1954 under contract first to MGM, then Columbia and then Warner Bros. By 1959 Moore's career was going cold. Under the terms of his contract, Warners had moved him on to television, giving him the lead in 'The Alaskans', now notorious as one of the worst television series ever made in Hollywood. From here Moore took over the *Maverick* role from James Garner before finally asking to be released from his contract. He returned to England in the spring of 1961.

Patrick McGoohan's name was also in the hat (he is said to have turned it down because of the sado-masochism evident in the role) but the 'smart' money was on established stars with the sort of polished upper-class image which the Bond role demanded – people like David Niven who, as indicated earlier, was Ian Fleming's first choice, Rex Harrison or Michael Redgrave.

Where an English producer might have been hidebound by English class traditions, Broccoli and Saltzman were both North Americans. Anyway, they did not want someone who was already a star. They wanted a comparative unknown, someone who would not argue about being signed up for five, six or seven Bond films.

By October 1961 Saltzman and Broccoli were still looking for their man, and were becoming desperate. Shooting had been delayed until the early months of 1962 and, beginning to panic, they arranged for the *Daily Express* to run a competition to find someone to fill the role. There were 1,100 replies from which they selected six finalists. These were screen tested at Twickenham studios and though one, a male model called Peter Anthony, was considered promising, the producers did not think him quite right for the Bond role. Terence Young had already been signed up as director and he recommended Sean Connery. Saltzman had seen Connery in *The Frightened City* and had been reasonably impressed. Broccoli had seen him in *Darby O'Gill and the Little People* and had made a mental note of his wife Dana's enthusiastic comments on the young Scots actor. They procured recordings of some of Connery's past appearances and watched them. According to Saltzman, Connery 'had suffered a small but fatal miscasting all the way down the line'. Still unsure, they called Richard Hatton and asked him to send Connery round.

Connery knew that Saltzman and Broccoli had optioned the rights to most of the existing novels. He also knew that production had been delayed while they scoured *Spotlight* for someone to play the leading role. It had been in the papers. As an article in *Kinematograph Weekly* reported in the summer of 1961: 'If the films are anything like as successful as the books, it will mean international stardom for whoever plays the title role. But it won't be an established star. The plan is to use a completely unknown actor.' The rumour in the business was that the budget would not stretch to paying a 'star' salary. If Connery was the one chosen, and if the Bond films took off, he reasoned, they had the potential to make him a major star. But he had been to auditions before and been disappointed. Promising ideas did not always make promising scripts and promising scripts did not always make good pictures – and, anyway, he might not get the part.

He had read one of the Bond novels, *Live and Let Die*, a few years previously, and he knew the character – or what there was of it. If the Bond films were a success he would be a rich man, and a younger Connery might have jumped in head first. But at the age of 31 he was mature enough to know that, despite the track records of Broccoli and Saltzman, the films could be an unmitigated disaster and he was astute enough to worry about the danger of typecasting.

In the offices of Eon Productions, Broccoli and Saltzman were waiting. Saltzman was the smaller of the two, more abrupt, more intense while Broccoli was of larger proportions, more gregarious, more jovial. Also in the room were George H. Ornstein, boss of United Artists' new London production office, and Stanley Sopel, the United Artists' accountant. Any moment now the door would open and in would walk the man who might become their urbane, sophisticated, upper-class James Bond.

Terence Young, knowing Connery's preference for casual

clothes, had telephoned him earlier to warn him to dress properly for the interview, to wear a suit and a shirt and tie. When the door did open, the man who walked in was good-looking, confident, muscular, his dark hair now thinning a little at the front. Connery sat down, and briefly their hearts sank. Slouched in the chair, wearing baggy trousers, suede shoes and a brown shirt open at the neck, he was about as far removed from anyone's mental picture of the upper-class secret agent as it was possible to get. He dressed 'deliberately to antagonize', Young was later to claim.

During the negotiations which followed, Connery was no push-over. He laid down his terms. He insisted that they let him star in two non-Bond films for every Bond film he made. He thumped the table to emphasize his demands. He refused to audition for the part on the basis that he could not possibly put across in a few moments the humour he knew was essential to the part. 'You either take me as I am or not at all,' he said. And when he left the offices the four in the room crowded round the window and watched him 'bounce' along towards his car. Even though Connery had not finally committed himself to the role, they knew they had found the man they wanted. Connery for his part wanted time to consider. He would talk to Diane, he would talk to Richard Hatton, he would take expert advice before he finally signed to do the films.

His first reaction to being offered the role was, he later admitted, one of surprise. Doubts then began to creep in. 'I could see that . . . it would be a marvellous opening,' he was to tell *Playboy* years later. 'But . . . I didn't think it would take off as it did. After I got over my first surprise and really began to consider it, I didn't want to do it because I could see that, properly made, it would have to be the first of a series and I wasn't sure I wanted to get involved in that and the constraints that go with it. Contracts choke you and I wanted to be free.'

But how could he turn it down? If the films came off they would make him wealthy and they would make him famous. 'He knew as well as we did that Bond was a real leading-man role,' said Harry Saltzman, 'one that went through the film from the first scene to the last scene.' If it all worked out, Saltzman and Broccoli had planned for him to do six films: *Dr*

No, From Russia with Love, Goldfinger, Thunderball, On Her Majes-
ty's Secret Service and *You Only Live Twice.*

The decision by Saltzman and Broccoli to give Sean Connery
the Bond role was extraordinary. Connery was unlike Bond in
almost every obvious respect: where Bond was elegant, Connery was unkempt; where Bond was suave, Connery was
unsophisticated; where Bond had an upper-class English
accent, Connery had a rich Scottish brogue; where Bond had
been educated at Eton and Fettes, Connery had left Darroch
Junior Secondary before his 14th birthday. Much has been
made of the fact that Bond was of Scottish extraction and had
been educated in his early years in Fettes, the most up-market
of all Edinburgh's public schools – just a mile or so across the
city from where Sean Connery was born and brought up.

But when Broccoli and Saltzman hired Connery to play
Bond, they were not interested in the trivia of his background.
What they *were* interested in was Connery's height and physical strength, his fearlessness, his animal grace, his panther-like
walk, his attractiveness to the opposite sex, even his acting – all
of which had combined to lend him an aggressive charm which
was to shine through in the Bond films (just as it had done in
Darby O'Gill and the Little People). He also had an unusual face –
good-looking but with just that touch of hardness and cruelty
that Fleming had written into Bond.

'Cubby and I went through 200 actors in 1961 before choos-
ing Sean,' Saltzman was to say later. 'We liked the way he
moved. Only one other actor moves as well, and that's Albert
Finney.' Broccoli was impressed by the way he had banged the
desk and set out his demands: 'He looked like he had balls.'

Fleming, by now completely disillusioned with the ins and
outs of showbiz, was enthusiastic when Saltzman phoned him
with the news. Despite rumours to the contrary, he had no
casting approval. According to his biographer John Pearson,
Connery was described to him in glowing terms: 'Saltzman
thinks he has found an absolute corker, a 30-year-old ex-
Shakespearian actor, ex-Navy boxing champion . . . even, he
says, intelligent. But . . . I am staying away from all this side of
the business.'

This is confirmed by Ivar Bryce in his biography of Ian
Fleming, *You Only Live Once*: 'A little-known Shakespearian

actor with a handsome head upon an athletic body, Sean Connery, was chosen. As is universally known, it turned out to be an inspired choice . . . in spite of early worries about the difficulty he had in modifying his Scottish accent.'

Though there is a degree of truth in Saltzman's description of Connery as an 'ex-Shakespearian actor', he is perhaps more to be admired for his hyperbole than his honesty. Connery had, indeed, played Hotspur in a couple of BBC television productions. He had also appeared in a version of *Macbeth* made for Canadian television, but to describe him as an ex-Shakespearian actor is perhaps to give an impression which was not quite deserved. In any case, when Fleming met the young actor, he was less than impressed. 'I was looking for Commander James Bond, not an overgrown stunt man,' was his withering remark. But his derision was to change to respect as he came to appreciate Connery's ability to bring humour and humanity to the Bond character.

On meeting Fleming, Connery was frank about the books. 'I told Ian Fleming that I thought the Bond books were marvellous. But the businessman in me knew that Bond, as Fleming wrote him, couldn't possibly succeed without a young audience. I said we'd have to play the character a bit more for laughs, bring a bit of fantasy in. Ian Fleming was a bit taken aback at first but he agreed.'

Connery got the Bond role in November 1961 and by the end of the year he was already warming to the sado-masochism for which the Bond films were to become famous. In an interview in the *Sunday Express* published on the last day of the year, he was to tell Susan Barnes: 'We Scots have a tremendous appreciation of the worlds of the devil,' referring, she recorded, in particular to himself and Ian Fleming (who was half Scottish).

'James Bond is very much for breaking the rules,' he went on. 'He enjoys freedom that the normal person doesn't get. He likes to eat. He likes to drink. He likes his girls. He is rather cruel, sadistic. He takes in a big percentage of the fantasies of lots of people – although it's difficult to get many of them to admit they'd like to be Bond. I have no compunction at all about admitting that I like to eat, I like to drink, I like girls.'

During the interview Connery made comments, for the first time, about violence towards women for which he was later to gain some notoriety. 'I don't think there's anything very wrong about hitting a woman,' Susan Barnes quotes him as saying. 'I don't though recommend hitting a woman the way you hit a man. An open-handed slap is justifiable. Or putting your hand over her mouth. But I wouldn't think I was sadistic.' Connery would hardly have believed that these comments, 30 years on, would have caused such a scandal that they would lead to questions in the Houses of Parliament.

Connery's major contribution is the humour he insisted on bringing to the part. As Ornstein observed: 'Anyone's ideas were welcomed and, if good, they were used.' As Broccoli put it: 'They are probably the only films written by committee.' Connery's Bond is an affable and fun-loving man – albeit with a fist of iron – far removed from the deliberately shallow and sophisticated Bond of Fleming's novels, who was little more than a hook on which the stories could be hung.

'Sean told me that the producers thought they could get away with doing it absolutely seriously,' says Frank Hauser, 'and that *he* was the one who said it had to be funny. And Sean wasn't a braggart by any means.'

One possible problem was that Connery did not have the background for the role. He did not know how the upper classes behaved, the clubs they attended, the clothes they wore. His own preference for casual slacks and open-necked shirts would not suit the Bond character nor his personal appearances as a representative of the film-makers. But he was in good hands. The film's director, Terence Young, born in Shanghai in 1915, the son of a police commissioner, had been educated at Harrow and Cambridge and served as a Guards officer during the war. He was a 'gentleman' of the old style who bought his suits in Savile Row, and what Connery lacked in urbane sophistication Young would give to him. As Stanley Sopel was later to observe: 'Terence Young created Bond in his own image.'

By the time Eon started filming, Connery was ready for the part. Every inch the urbane sophisticated gentleman complete with bespoke tailored suits, his Scottish accent was modulated with upper-class inflexions (though not entirely obliterated) while his mannerisms were those of an English gent and his receding hairline was enhanced by a black toupee.

Dr No was shot on location in Jamaica and at Pinewood studios north of London. The film is about one Dr Julius No, an evil man who, from his hide-out on the isolated Jamaican island of Crab Key, was beaming confusing signals to missiles being launched from Cape Canaveral. As a result the missiles were either crashing into the sea or going dangerously off course. Bond's mission was to search and destroy. This is achieved after avoiding death by the bite of a deadly tarantula, after being shot in bed by Dr No's henchman and after a series of adventures during which he is forced into a lethal obstacle course devised by No which, remarkably, he survives. He then manages to kill Dr No (in the book, by submerging him under a huge heap of guano) and he and the obligatory nubile beauty, Honeychile Rider, make their escape.

Work began on January 1962 and filming was completed by March. 'No one gave *Dr No* much hope of success,' Connery was to say later. 'I was an unknown, the co-producer Cubby Broccoli was not an international name and we were projecting an English secret agent as a super-hero. There were times when the director, Terence Young, and I were on location and both thinking, what on earth have we here? Will anyone want to watch?' Initially, their worries were confirmed. Executives of United Artists in America, flown over for a special showing, were less than impressed. One is reported to have quipped: 'Well, all we can lose is $950,000', another to have refused to handle a film with 'a truck driver' in the lead. As a result, the distributors decided not to promote the film in the States.

Even without promotion, there was no hiding its success. According to Shelley Winters in her autobiography, Connery took her to the première of the film when it was released in the States. 'He was very nervous about the film; in fact he hated it.' But by the time the screening had finished, such was the crush of reporters wanting to talk to him that it took them 15 minutes to fight their way to the exit. 'When we . . . came out of the theater that night,' says Winters, 'Sean was a superstar.'

Diane Cilento agreed. 'Well, Sean is a star. There's no doubt about that,' she told Frank Hauser in a telephone conversation just after *Dr No* had been released. Hauser had doubts about Cilento's impartiality. 'But the moment you saw him in that film, you thought: "Yup, that's someone who has presence and nerve."'

Not everyone was as enthusiastic. The reviewer from the *Daily Telegraph* struggled to find anything good to say about it, managing only: 'Sean Connery plays this prize phoney (Bond) as convincingly as any actor could who does not stand 6ft 6in in his socks.' *Variety* reviewed the film as 'An entertaining piece of tongue-in-cheek action hokum' while *Films and Filming* spoke of '. . . the headiest box-office concoction of sex and sadism ever brewed up in a British studio . . .'. But box-office receipts confirmed the view of Winters, Cilento and Hauser. It was to be the second best box-office attraction in 1962 (this, despite the fact that it was released in October) and was to go on playing to packed houses until well into 1963. It broke box-office records at cinemas all over Britain. Within 14 weeks of its release it had taken a record $10 million.

Just a few weeks after the release of *Dr No*, Connery married Cilento, already heavy with their son Jason. Her divorce from André Volpe had just come through and she and Connery knew well enough the scandal that was likely to break if they married in London. The wedding, on 29 November 1962 in the Registry Office on the Rock of Gibraltar, was delayed because Cilento, arriving on the Rock separately from the Spanish mainland, had problems with her Australian passport. When the problems were sorted out, the ceremony was witnessed by two local taxi drivers and the newly weds spent the night in the Rock Hotel before motoring off for a honeymoon on the Costa del Sol.

Many who knew Cilento, whose daughter Giovanna from her marriage to André Volpe, was now four years old, were astonished at news of the wedding. Diane, five years younger than Connery, had told them that she was not cut out for marriage and assured them that she would not marry again. As she herself told Patricia Barry of *The People* in 1969, shortly before she and Connery were to split up: 'I didn't want to get married. Having been married and made a bodge of it, I didn't rate marriage. I thought it was too stifling. Sean did talk me round. He was sure we could make a go of it.'

Her pregnancy too had helped change her mind and, despite

the fact that she had been brought up in a markedly more privileged environment than Sean, she was well liked in Fountainbridge – which Connery still visited whenever he was able – and got on well with the family. Whereas Julie Hamilton had never really been able to communicate with Effie and Joe, Diane's first move on being taken up to the flat at 176 Fountainbridge was to flop back in an armchair, kick off her shoes and start talking to Sean's parents as if she had been brought up in the next street. Following the birth of their son Jason, neighbours remember them well walking up and down Fountainbridge with the boy in a buggy. Connery refused to break his ties with the old place. His old friends in Edinburgh still remember him standing them a pint at Foy's Bar on Fountainbridge whenever he was in town to visit his parents.

Jason Connery was born on 11 January 1963 in Rome. Back in London they found a nanny for him and started decorating the three-storey 12-bedroom ex-nunnery, Adoratrices House, that Connery had bought in Centre Avenue near the park in Acton, west London, through the company his accountant had earlier advised him to set up, Sean Connery Ltd. (later the Sean Connery Company Ltd.).

Though he was still anxious to do 'serious' acting, he was realistic about the value of the Bond role. It had already earned him £15,000 for a couple of months' work and there would be more of the same to come. 'I cannot ignore the commercial value of James Bond,' he told a journalist. 'The reason I want to do James Bond is to enable me to do more serious work. It puts me in a stronger position to do this. That is really all it means. After all, I have been in many serious plays.'

In the same interview he explained why he refused to adopt the traditional 'English' accent, preferring to hang on to the Scottish brogue which had caused such comment in the past and which had led to a goodly number of Irish roles on stage and television. 'I have had speech training, voice production and all that. But I like my accent and I refuse to speak what some people call "English".'

Over the next few years the Bond films were to be made and released at yearly intervals and Sean Connery was to become increasingly famous and increasingly strongly associated in the public mind with the Bond role. The second Bond film, made and released in 1963, was *From Russia with Love* for which United Artists put up $2 million and which was promoted strongly in America following President Kennedy's revelation that the book on which it was based was in his personal top ten. It was Kennedy's endorsement of the book, according to Alan Whicker, which 'made Connery, an unknown actor, the most famous face in the world'.

This followed the same all-sex all-action format of *Dr No*. It opens at a chess championship in Venice where we find that SPECTRE, an independent world-wide criminal organization, is planning an operation against the Russians involving the unwitting 'help' of the British Secret Service in the shape of James Bond. The action moves to Istanbul, where Bond meets the beautiful Tatiana (played by Daniella Bianchi), who has allegedly fallen in love with him through a photograph. Bond is after a Russian cypher machine to which he believes Tatiana may lead him. With her help, Bond steals the machine from the Russian embassy and boards the train for Venice. But now SPECTRE are after him. On the train they try to kill Bond and steal the cypher machine and Bond uses the technology provided by the British Secret Service together with his own wits and abilities to prevent both of these things happening. Bond and Tatiana leave the train and hijack a truck. After shooting down a helicopter in the sky and taking to the water in a speedboat, the couple is confronted by a female agent of SPECTRE. Tanya shoots her and the action moves back to Venice, Bond and Tanya in a gondola, happy ever after.

Location filming for *From Russia with Love* was done in Turkey and Sean took Diane along with him. By now he was becoming known as a stickler for professionalism, always arriving on time, always well prepared, always word-perfect with his lines – and expecting a similar degree of preparation from his fellow professionals. He was annoyed when *From Russia with Love* overran its shooting schedule (not to mention its budget).

When released, the film enjoyed the distinction of being the first film ever to be shown at four West End cinemas simultaneously. It was received by the viewing public with enthusiasm. Even the soundly conservative *Daily Telegraph*, found it 'morally safer' than *Dr No*, the gratuitous sex and sadism having been 'toned down'.

In 1964 the third Bond movie, *Goldfinger*, financed by United Artists to the tune of $3 million and directed by Guy Hamilton, was released amid a welter of publicity both in the UK and the States. Here the villain, one Auric Goldfinger, has spent the past 15 years devising a plan to set off an atomic bomb amidst the gold reserves in Fort Knox, rendering the gold radioactive and thus boosting the value of his own gold, and at the same time bringing the economies of the West to the brink of disaster. Once again, Bond's investigations involve him in certain death, this time from a laser beam, but he miraculously escapes in time to defuse the bomb and thus ruin Goldfinger's plans. Goldfinger meets his death during a mid-air fight with Bond. A bullet pierces the cabin window and, during the sudden depressurization, he is sucked out.

The Bond roller-coaster, which had started moving with *From Russia with Love*, hit new heights with the release of *Goldfinger*. Financially, it was to become the most successful Bond film of all and even Connery had managed to negotiate a better deal for himself, with £50,000 up front and a percentage of the profits.

Variety's review reflected Terence Young's influence: 'Connery repeats his suave portrayal of the punch-packing Bond, who can find his way round the wine list as easily as he can negotiate a dame.' Reviewing the film for the *Observer*, Penelope Gilliatt observed that 'the tone of the Bond pictures isn't really at all like the tone of Ian Fleming's books. It is more self-mocking and in a horrific way more elegant.' She continued, prophetically, 'we may look back . . . 20 years from now and . . . realize . . . this was the brassy, swinging, ungallant taste that the Sixties left on the tongue.'

Goldfinger was also to become one of the most successful films ever made in Britain, yet its star, Sean Connery, the man who was well on his way to *becoming* James Bond to half the world, was not at the London première. Instead, he was in Almeria, Spain, shooting *The Hill*. He was already tiring of Bond and of all the publicity which surrounded it. His dislike of journalists was growing and he was becoming impatient and bad-tempered with them. This was leading to accusations of arrogance, indeed, accusations which he and his close friends knew to be grossly unfair. He was simply fed up of answering the same questions time and again and of talking to journalists who had not carried out their research properly. He was later to tell the story of how, during the filming of *Goldfinger*, the publicity man left him alone with a French lady journalist. 'First of all she asked me what the film was called, then what part I was playing; then she asked who was starring opposite me. I said a very famous German actor called Gert Frobe. "Well, I've never heard of her," she said, and with that I just blew up and walked off the set.'

He was also becoming increasingly disillusioned with the Bond character. By the time *Goldfinger* had been shot, he felt that he had made all he could make of it. He had milked it dry, had taken it as far as it would go and the rest was mechanical. He was internationally known, he had money; now he could do as he pleased.

Or could he?

The previous year had seen the emergence into public life of the Beatles. The term 'Beatlemania' was coined to describe the adulation of their fans, and it was with the release of *Goldfinger* that 'Bondmania' began to break out in earnest and Connery began to receive the sort of adulation previously accorded only to pop stars. 'At least there were four of them to share it,' he later remarked. 'The Bond thing was very difficult to handle. You can't imagine the demand for pictures and interviews. Anybody who hasn't been under that pressure cannot know what it's like.'

His long-time friend Michael Caine, in his own auto-biography *What's It All About* mentions 'several conversations' he had with Connery 'in which he expressed his fear that the Bond character was now so popular that he was beginning to lose his own identity as an actor. Sean was afraid that this would make it difficult to get any other roles in the future.' Caine also recounts that when his own film *The Ipcress File* was being shown at Cannes, Connery flew in to see it but 'was so engulfed by the press and autograph hunters that he literally could not go to the hotel dining-room for a meal and so left the same day he had arrived, before the film was shown.'

Connery's dissatisfaction with the Bond role, fuelled partly by the natural anathema of this solitary and private man for publicity, partly by his feeling that the adoring fans did not understand the difficulties he had overcome in creating Bond as a screen character and partly by his conviction that the producers were underpaying him, began to boil over. He had been paid £6,000 for *Dr No*, only slightly more for *From Russia with Love* and £50,000 plus a small percentage of the profits for *Goldfinger*. In view of his role in 'creating' the character – a role that was recognized in 1964 by a Variety Club award – and also the millions of dollars that the producers were making for the pictures, he considered that his earnings were not enough. Like *From Russia with Love*, *Goldfinger* was shown in four West End cinemas simultaneously and, according to an article in *Films and Filming* the following year, had by then 'grossed far in excess of £10,000,000'. As Terence Young was later to observe: 'There they were, Cubby and Harry, sitting on $50 million or so and Sean outside the door calculating that maybe a third of it should be his.' Not everyone agreed, however. As American gossip columnist Sheilah Graham put it: 'Mr Connery . . . actually believes that Mr Saltzman and his partner, Cubby Broccoli, held back his career. He also believes they should have paid him more because he feels he alone is responsible for his success. And yet, before he played Bond, Sean was almost unknown as an actor . . .'

The pressures which superstardom put on Connery's relationship with Diane Cilento were extreme and were now testing it to breaking-point. Part of the problem is one common to show-business marriages: they were both busy actors, seeing each other only when their paths crossed. But a bigger part was the extremes of attention paid to Connery by the press, the fallout from which irked the Australian 'wild child'. Cilento was a rebel, an action woman. She had talent, abundant talent, and she knew it. She had good looks, painfully good looks, and she did not care. She was an actor par excellence and she wanted to be recognized for her own abilities. But she was becoming Mrs Sean Connery. People would ring up and ask if she was Mrs James Bond. Journalists would request interviews and then quiz her ˑfor hours about her life with Sean Connery. The problem was that, in the eyes of the public, Sean Connery had become James Bond – and Diane was an accessory after the fact. Amidst all the pressures, under the constant scrutiny of the public gaze, the relationship snapped and Connery moved out, leaving Diane Cilento and the children in the house in Acton.

In her interview with Patricia Barry of *The People* in 1969, three years after Connery had given up the Bond role, she still felt the need to grumble about the problems caused by Bondmania. 'Make no mistake about it, the 007 bit was great for Sean. Hell, we've made a packet out of it. But, oh, it was so boring for Sean. And you know, you have to be pretty strong-willed to hold on to your own identity against a character like 007. Once you get a screen image it's a murderous thing to keep out of your private life. Everyone expects Sean to be womanizing like crazy all the time. Sitting at home with the kids just isn't on.'

The fourth Bond film, *Thunderball*, was preceded by a court case Kevin McClory had raised against Ian Fleming and his friend Ivar Bryce for breach of copyright. Bryce was financing the defence. McClory argued in court that ideas put forward by himself and Jack Whittingham were used by Fleming in the book *Thunderball*. After ten long days in 1963, Bryce decided to give up the case and as Fleming, despite the success of the Bond books, could not afford to continue the case on his own, a settlement was announced in open court. The figure which changed hands was not disclosed, but was believed to be in the region of £35,000, not an inconsiderable sum in those days, and was paid by Bryce. Fleming also agreed that the novel was based on a screen treatment devised by himself, McClory and Whittingham and, in return for a payment, forsook the film rights to the novel and also his interest in the screenplay. In return, McClory forsook any interest in the novel itself (though subsequent paperback editions contained the disclaimer 'Based on a screen treatment by Kevin McClory, Jack Whittingham and Ian Fleming').

When the dust had settled on the case, filming of *Thunderball* began. The story centres around SPECTRE's arch-villain Ernst Blofeld's theft of a UK nuclear bomber which has been ditched in the Atlantic, its bombs taken and hidden on a remote island. These are to be returned on payment of a huge ransom or SPECTRE will explode them in a Western city. Bond and underwater agents find the bomber on the seabed in Nassau, but the bombs have gone. Using a geiger counter hidden in a watch and an underwater infra-red camera, Bond finds the bombs aboard a yacht and after a battle with Blofeld's henchman, retrieves them for his masters.

When Connery flew out for the location shooting in The Bahamas, he gave only one interview, to journalists from *Playboy* magazine whom he had met over drinks a few weeks earlier in London, despite being besieged by the international press. Even with them he was curt. Asked about the problems of typecasting, he replied: 'Let me straighten you out on this. The problem in interviews of this sort is to get across the fact, without breaking your arse, that one is *not* Bond. There are a lot of things I did before Bond – like playing the classics on stage – that don't seem to get publicized. So you see this Bond image is a problem in a way and a bit of a bore, but one has just got to live with it.'

By this time reconciliation between himself and Diane was on the cards, and Diane flew out to Nassau, with Jason and Giovanna, then three and eight respectively, in tow. It was there, during the long idle days when Connery was away shooting the action scenes for the film, that she started work on the first of her two novels, *The Manipulator*. This told of the underhand goings-on during one day and one night of an international film festival in Acapulco, Mexico. The villain of the book was one Nicholas Jebs, the manipulator himself, who, according to the cover blurb 'knew everything, he knew everyone. He pried into the chinks in their armour, stabbed the flesh and twisted the knife. From the nymphomaniac starlets and the sex-crazed stars to the disillusioned writers and the world-weary directors – all came under Jeb's spell. But there was one man in the cast who was immune to Jeb's plans. For him, film festivals were as effete as sackcloth and ashes.' The book came out in 1967 and the dedication page ran simply 'For Sean'.

In December 1965 *Thunderball* was released and by the end of the year was top film in America and the second most popular in Britain, beaten only by *The Sound of Music*. As *Variety* said:

'Connery is his usual stylish self as he lives up to past rep, in which mayhem is a casual affair.'

While the dreams of Fleming, Saltzman and Broccoli were realized in full, for Connery, the part was played out. It had offered him fame and money and now he had these in abundance. He was tired of the role, tired of the adulation, and he was planning to quit. But the Bond films had offered him one unexpected benefit: golf. This was no childhood passion instilled into him on the municipal golf courses of Edinburgh. The plot of *Goldfinger* specifically stated that Bond played golf – off a handicap of nine. 'I took the game up . . . only because I had to look the part for the golfing scenes inseparable from the James Bond role in *Goldfinger*.' With his usual thoroughness he took professional lessons at Stoke Poges – 'but not all that many' – and has been entranced with the game ever since. 'I was once asked whether I would rather win an Oscar or the Open. I unhesitatingly nominated the latter.'

The fifth Bond film was *You Only Live Twice*. The plot involves a dispute between the Americans and the Russians about the destruction of an American spacecraft. The British have evidence to suggest that it was not done by the Russians and that the rocket responsible came down in the seas around Japan. Bond is sent there to investigate where he is helped by Tiger Tanaka, head of the Japanese Secret Service. Tanaka has Bond taught in the martial art of *ninja* and instructs him to marry a Japanese girl, Kissy Suzuki, to help his cover. Eventually Bond comes face-to-face for the first time with SPECTRE arch-villain Blofeld (who played a key role in *Thunderball*) in his operations headquarters, a volcanic crater with a sliding roof through which he launches his rockets. Although another rocket has just been launched, Bond defeats Blofeld (who escapes to fight another day) and causes the rocket to self-destruct seconds before it causes the start of World War III.

This film was, for Connery, the straw which broke the camel's back. It was to be filmed in 1966 and released the following year, and in July of 1966 when he arrived in Tokyo with Diane to start location shooting, Bondmania took off all over again. As Michael Caine was to observe later in an interview recorded by Scottish Television, 'You can't, unless you have a massive, massive hit like that, make international stardom. With an action film you become famous in every nation in the world.'

The journey itself, planned as a holiday for Sean and Diane, was a disaster from the start. His fame had spread to all quarters of the globe and he and Diane were mobbed by fans in Bangkok when they stopped off there on their way to Tokyo, and again in Manila. At Tokyo Airport they were mobbed again. By the time they arrived at the Tokyo Hilton, where they were to spend their first night in Japan, they were once again victims of the press and Broccoli had quickly to arrange a press conference to satisfy their curiosity. James Bond was as popular in the east as he was in the west and with filming to be done on location there, excitement was at fever pitch.

But Connery was tired and irritable on his arrival in Tokyo. He appeared at the press conference in an open-necked shirt and slacks, minus his socks and his toupee. Never the most diplomatic of men, he became brutally blunt. Asked at the press conference if he liked Japanese women, he replied: 'Japanese women are just not sexy. This is even more so when they hide their figures by wearing these roomy kimonos.' Asked what he did when his children misbehaved, he replied: 'I beat them.'

At the same press conference, he announced his intention to retire from the Bond role. He had asked Broccoli and Saltzman if he could be released from his contract with one film, *On Her Majesty's Secret Service*, still to go and they let him go, convinced that they could find someone who could do the job equally well and possibly for less money. Their only proviso was that he would carry out his obligations for *You Only Live Twice*. 'It started as a joke,' was how Connery described the Bond films, 'but things got out of hand – everything became magnified . . . It is important for any actor to play diverse roles,' he said. 'The final straw was *You Only Live Twice*. That took six months of my time – and that on top of two or three postponements. I could never give a firm date to anyone else and that meant I missed out on other parts I wanted to do.'

Once the press conference was over, Connery asked Broccoli if, during their one night in Tokyo – they were flying out for location filming in Kyushu the next day – they could see something of Japan. Broccoli quickly organized an outing to a small exclusive restaurant across town and two cars to take them there. The subterfuge which followed was in itself worthy of a James Bond movie. According to broadcaster Alan Whicker, who was with the party filming an episode of *Whicker's World* for television, Broccoli, Connery and the others tiptoed from Broccoli's suite – aptly No 1007 – to the service lift which took them to the underground garage where the cars were ready, engines running. Unfortunately, in the street outside, they were spotted by an eagle-eyed photographer and as a result they were pursued through the streets of Tokyo by five carloads of Japanese photographers, cameras at the ready, all determined to get that exclusive photograph of *Bondo-san*, 'Mr Bond' in Japanese. Once they reached the restaurant it was little better as first one, then another photographer-disguised-as-diner had to be forcibly ejected. 'In Japan,' says Whicker, 'no one could escape the instant impact of Bondmania.'

As if to punish him for his decision to forsake the role for more serious parts, the location filming presented numerous problems. Everywhere he went he was pursued by cameramen and reporters – he was even followed into the lavatories. The insects were a constant irritation. And the heat was so intense – 'working in that steam-heat was like moving through a Turkish bath', according to Alan Whicker – that he suffered from dehydration. 'I was slowing down without realizing it,' Connery was to say later. 'They had to pump a pint of saline into me.'

According to Alan Whicker, Connery seemed to have 'abandoned his fierce professional concentration' and seemed indifferent to the film's progress. 'At Pinewood I noticed he retreated to his dressing-room whenever possible . . . to practise putting.' Despite its star's lack of interest, *You Only Live Twice* was massively popular, and its première, in the Odeon, Leicester Square, on 12 June 1967, was the only one Connery attended in Britain. *Variety's* critic wrote that 'Sean Connery plays 007 with his usual finesse . . .'

For Connery, his success followed him everywhere he went. Crowds would gather outside the house in Acton Park, gazing in the front windows. He would be mobbed as soon as he walked down the garden path. Even the four walls of the house did not afford him the privacy he required. 'We have a marvellous house in Acton in a wonderful situation – a cul-de-sac right by the park,' he told Alan Whicker, 'but there are some real head-cases around. They just come up and sit on top of their cars, or knock at the door and say it would be marvellous if they could come in and have tea, or take some photographs or stand on your wall. There's only one way to solve it and that's not to be there.'

His popularity had other unpleasant effects. The house in Acton was burgled several times, the first time just after he had moved in. He was away on business, and four small boys aged nine and ten walked in off the street and made off with £50 worth of his property, including two cameras, an alarm clock, an electric razor and 16 records. In 1965 the house was broken into again and £300 worth of Diane's jewellery was taken along with a shotgun and cartridges. Tired of all the media attention, and conscious all the time of the risk from intruders, Connery and Cilento moved to a Victorian house at 1 Bristol Gardens, Portsmouth Road in Putney, the garden of which afforded them more privacy.

With the release of *You Only Live Twice*, Bond's – and Connery's – popularity had reached new heights. By the end of 1967, *The Times*, reporting on 'the success of British films in the American market', noted the results of a poll conducted by *Motion Picture Exhibitor* in America. 'Again, James Bond has carried all competition before him ... *Thunderball* being named Top Action Picture of the Year and Sean Connery Top Action Star.' By the following year he had been voted most popular film actor for the fourth year running in a poll conducted by *Motion Picture Herald*.

But Connery was never at his best with the trappings of superstardom. Diana Dors records in her *Diana Dors' A–Z of Men* the occasion in May 1966 that he accompanied her to the Muhammed Ali versus Henry Cooper world championship boxing match at Arsenal Stadium in North London. The pair were among a group of celebrities in the 45,000 crowd and, before the match began, had spent time signing for the numerous autograph hunters. 'Barely half-way through the first round, a woman suddenly came rushing up to Sean and I and shoved a book under our noses to sign, completely obscuring our view. Had she offered it to me first I suppose I would have laboriously agreed . . .' But unfortunately for the poor woman she shoved it under the nose of Connery.

'"Get out of my way, bloody woman," he snapped. "Do you think I've paid fifty quid a seat to sit here and look at you?"'

Connery's growing impatience was confirmed by Diane Cilento, speaking to Alan Whicker on the set of *You Only Live Twice*. 'He's not changed much because of Bond though perhaps nowadays he's quicker tempered because of all the pressures . . . He's tried beyond normal limits because everywhere you go there's always someone coming out from behind a tree.'

About their marriage itself Cilento was more enthusiastic, but only slightly. In her 1969 interview with Patricia Barry of *The People* she said: 'More than anything else I think marriage has helped me to develop as a person. Sean and I have both benefited mentally,' but 'I don't know whether I will be married five years from now. I cannot look that far into the future, for I like to live day by day.' Her words were prophetic: in six years' time Sean Connery would be marrying someone else.

Patricia Barry's article finished with an observation which may have said more than she realized about the relationship between Cilento and Connery: 'But before Diane could convince me any further what an independent soul she is, Sean appeared in the doorway asking, a little petulantly, for his lunch. And in five seconds flat Diane was on her feet and in the kitchen attending to it.' The free spirit of the fifties had become the dutiful wife of the sixties.

To help them get away from the pressures of Connery's superstardom, he and Diane had bought a smallholding near Marbella on Spain's Costa del Sol. It was a *hacienda* with a few acres of land close to a couple of top-class golf courses – Alalaya and Guadalmina. 'It all sounds terribly gooey,' Diane told Patricia Barry, 'but we sit and write together.' She was working on her second novel, *Hybrid*, while Sean was pursuing a long-term ambition, to write a film script for *Macbeth*. 'I sit at one end of the garden. And Sean sits at the other. Then every so often we toddle over to each other to show what we have done.'

A smaller house on the grounds was owned by Connery's

close friend and golfing partner Iain Stewart, a Scottish indus-trialist, who used to spend weeks there each summer with his wife and his teenage son Max. Max Stewart has fond memories of Diane Cilento: 'She was a wonderful woman, very attractive, very intelligent and very artistic. She ran a lovely house out there. The garden was perfect. There were lovely things about the house. She was a wonderful hostess.'

Diane's multiple talents stretched to skilled gardening; she spent her time in Spain digging irrigation ditches to bring water into the garden from a nearby river, planting vines for wine-making, growing grapefruits, melons, corn, decorating boxes with shells she had gathered from the Mediterranean beaches. But the cracks in their relationship were beginning to appear again. 'They would lead two quite separate lives,' says Max Stewart. 'I think there was something brewing at the time.'

At the start of the seventies, Connery's marriage to Diane Cilento finally hit the rocks. Jason and Giovanna were away at boarding-school at the time and so were shielded from the worst of the breakup, but even so, Jason has hard memories.

'It took about a year for them to break up and during that time there were many rows,' he said later. 'It was terribly upsetting. I realized just how much two people can hurt each other.' Connery moved out again, this time to a flat on Chelsea Embankment, and Diane, after the Putney house was sold, to a commune in New Malden, Surrey.

Meanwhile, Broccoli and Saltzman were trying to lure Con-nery back to play Bond in *Diamonds Are Forever*. They had cast the unknown Australian model George Lazenby in the role in the sixth Bond film *On Her Majesty's Secret Service* and though it had yielded a fair income of $38 million, it had been a slow starter. It had earned less than *You Only Live Twice* which, for its part, had earned less than *Thunderball*. By all accounts Lazenby had been 'difficult' to work with, had had ideas which, to Broccoli and Saltzman, were above his station. They knew that with Connery back, the cinema-goers would be out in force again. There were other problems too. In 1967 Gregory Ratoff's film version of *Casino Royale* had finally been released. The film had been directed in part by John Huston, who was later to direct Connery in *The Man Who Would Be King*, and contained a host of famous names – David Niven (finally getting the role for which he had been so heavily tipped in the 1960s), Deborah Kerr, Orson Welles, Peter Sellers, Ursula Andress, Woody Allen and George Raft as well as Scots actors Ronnie Corbett and Duncan Macrae. Ratoff had purchased the film rights for the book in the fifties and had hung on to them, grimly waiting for the opportunity to make use of them. Now with four Bond pictures already made, and the style well and truly set, he judged it time to do a spoof Bond, an elaborate and expensive piece of mickey-taking. It was an unmitigated disaster, described later by the veteran film critic Leslie Halliwell as 'one of the most shameless wastes of time and talent in screen history'. It had also put the wind up Broccoli and Saltzman, worried that the general public would miss the distinction between their James Bond and Ratoff's version.

Speaking to a journalist from the *Guardian* just two days before the film was released at the Odeon, Leicester Square, Connery had harsh words to say about George Lazenby and the director of *On Her Majesty's Secret Service*, Peter Hunt: 'Poor Lazenby just didn't have the experience, even though the director, Peter Hunt, was quoted as saying that he had taught Lazenby all he knew. And in three months! Lazenby couldn't do a good job because you have to have technique to get the character right. I know he behaved like a prize shit, alienating people so they tell me, though I've never met him, but it wasn't all his fault.'

He also had harsh words for the producers of the Bond films. 'For every good idea Harry (Saltzman) has had, he's gone on to eight flops.' And of Saltzman's relationship with Broccoli: 'They're not exactly enamoured of each other. Probably because they're both sitting on 50 million dollars or pounds and looking across the desk at each other and thinking that bugger's got half of what should be all mine.'

As Connery was reluctant to assume the mantle of Bond again, he held off Broccoli and Saltzman for a while, but finally agreed, planning to use a major chunk of his fee to finance an educational charity – the Scottish International Education Trust – that he had set up with friends in Scotland, and flew out of London at the beginning of 1971 to start filming in Las Vegas.

'I went back to do *Diamonds* only because I did it on my

terms and I got the kind of money I thought one should have had. And I had it paid before I did the movie.'

For taking part in the film, his hard bargain had included a 'large percentage' of the profits and also that if the film ran over schedule he would be paid an extra £40,000 for every week it overran. It ran to schedule. He also made the distributors, United Artists, promise that they would distribute two other films – of his choice – to be made by his own production company, Tantallon Films; this had been set up in 1971 and represented a long-term ambition.

The plot of *Diamonds Are Forever* centres yet again on arch-villain Blofeld. This time he has devised another way of holding the world to ransom, using a giant orbiting laser beam whose energies are concentrated by stolen diamonds and which can cause rockets, missiles and submarines to self-destruct. He is prepared to sell it to the highest bidder, who will then have nuclear supremacy. Bond is sent to Las Vegas to investigate. His wife, Tracy, had been murdered by Blofeld in the previous film (Lazenby's *On Her Majesty's Secret Service*) and he is out for revenge. He causes Blofeld's miniature submarine to blow up while the arch-villain is supposedly still inside.

Diamonds Are Forever was released at the end of 1971 to favourable reviews. *The Times* called it 'the major offering' of 1971's last week and observed that it was bringing back 'the only proper screen James Bond, Sean Connery'. The result, it went on, 'is not exactly tops in the Bond film canon, but is more than enjoyable enough to be going on with.' Typically, the highbrow *Films and Filming* was unenthusiastic. According to their reviewer, Connery returned to the Bond role 'as blandly as his admirers could possibly wish'. But as anticipated the film was a box-office smash and Connery, at the centre once again of the whole Bond business, vowed yet again that he would never do another Bond picture.

Years later he was to say: 'You could never tell when you were going to finish and that put me in a very vulnerable position in terms of wanting to do other pictures. I was involved in *You Only Live Twice* for six months while *From Russia with Love* took 18 weeks. When the time came to do *Diamonds Are Forever*, I put a limitation on it.'

Besides demands placed on him by the nature of the Bond

role itself, not to mention the publicity involved, typecasting was becoming a problem as he had envisaged at the outset. He found it was getting to the stage where people were unable to appreciate him in other roles and this was restricting, intolerably restricting.

'But the general public wanted to see me doing Bond because they liked the movies so much. Even when I went away and came back, they still wanted to see them.

'The opportunities to do interesting stuff that could compete with the success of the Bond films were few. It was always my intention to do other films, but I was contracted for the Bonds.' And if he was required for the Bonds, the Bonds took precedence over anything else.

'No film you could do, no matter how good it was, could possibly compete with the next James Bond film. It was very frustrating.'

It is often noted, not without surprise, that Connery's incredible success as James Bond did not change him, did not leave him conceited. Scottish writer William McIlvanney confirms this. He met Connery in the lobby of the Dorchester Hotel on Park Lane in the late sixties, having been asked by the *Observer* to write an article about him. At the time Connery was concerned about his brother Neil, a plasterer by trade, who had just been involved in the making of the film *Operation Kid Brother*, a comic spoof in which James Bond's brother defeats an international mastermind with the aid of a Scottish archery team. Neil, he told McIlvanney, would have to make up his mind whether he was an actor or a plasterer. McIlvanney found Connery 'very straight, but very hard – in a good way. He has a combination of kindness and authority which is very powerful. He's somebody who looks as if his body fits him.' He remembers that Connery paid for the drinks and left a tip which was reasonable, not outrageous, a Tommy Connery tip, not a James Bond one. In the finished article, which the *Observer* never used, he was to describe Connery as 'an interestingly hand-knitted commodity in an industry of synthetic fibres'.

The Bond films created a genre of their own, and Connery had a unique place in the creation of that genre. The James

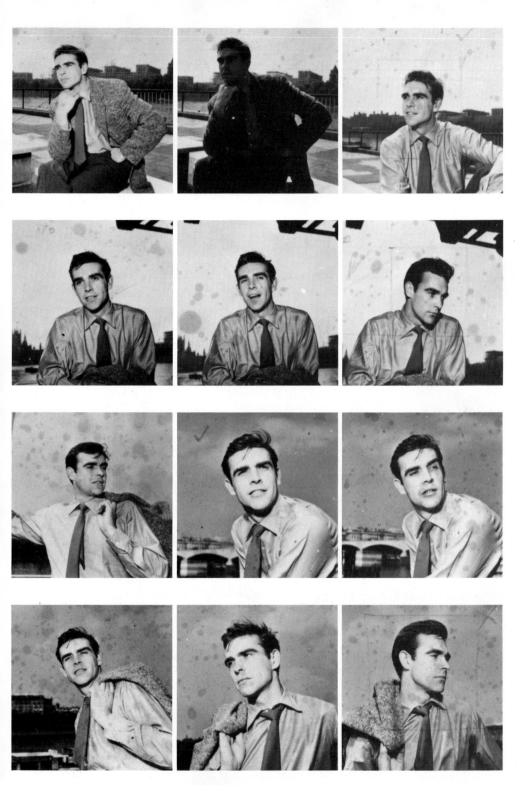

The first set of pictures Connery had taken professionally when he decided to pursue a career as an actor.

Kenny Edwards with his brother during a party at the Connerys'
Fountainbridge flat. Sean Connery's father Joe is in the background.

Connery with Kenny Edwards's brother.

Signing autographs in
his parents' Fountainbridge
flat, 1958.

Connery's class at Tollcross Primary School in Fountainbridge which he attended from 1935 to 1937. Young Tommy Connery is third from the right, third row back.

Fetlor Athletic was just one of the junior league football teams Connery played for as a teenager. He is third from right in the middle row.

Big Tam with friends at the Portobello Pool in Edinburgh. Connery has his arm round Sheila MacLean. Val Volante is on the extreme left of the picture, and Jimmy Lawrie on the extreme right.

Again at the Portobello Pool.

With Val Volante's father outside
Ritchie's restaurant in Cockburn Street.

With Kenny Edwards and his children
outside the Fountainbridge tenement.

With Val Volante and Val Volante's mother, again in Cockburn Street.

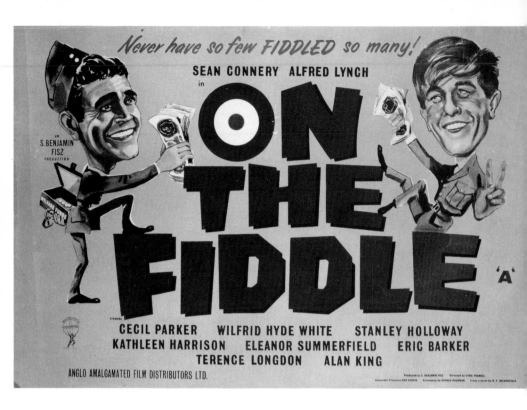

Publicity material from two of Connery's earliest films.

With Tippi Hedren in Hitchcock's *Marnie*.

With Brigitte Bardot in *Shalako*.

With Ursula Andress in *Dr No*.

Relaxing on location with his first wife Diane Cilento during the filming of *Thunderball*, 1965.

With Ian Fleming on the set of *From Russia with Love*, 1963.

With Bond producer Albert R. Broccoli during the filming of *Diamonds Are Forever*.

With Michelle Pfeiffer on location
during the filming of *The Russia House*.

With Audrey Hepburn, with whom he
co-starred in *Robin and Marian*.

On location with Kevin Costner during the filming of *The Untouchables*.

Arriving in Edinburgh in 1991 with his wife Micheline Roquebrune to receive the Freedom of the City of Edinburgh.

Micheline was reportedly upset by Connery's lingering screen kiss with Barbara Carrera in *Never Say Never Again*.

Connery with Micheline, his brother Neil, his sister-in-law and, on the left, Eleanor McLaughlin who nominated him for the Freedom of the City of Edinburgh.

Pursuing one of his favourite pastimes.

Bond character of the books was two-dimensional and it was Connery who fattened it out, who made it real – so much so that as early as 1964 he received an award from the Variety Club of Great Britain for 'creating' James Bond. The films may have had their faults, but they were well crafted and the formula was right.

As Ian Johnson observed in *Films and Filming* just before the release of *Thunderball*: 'Anybody can . . . pick fault with the Bond films – the chase sequence in *Goldfinger* was better done by the Keystone Cops, Hitchcock held suspense better, *The Big Sleep* and *Secret Agent* threw more caution to the winds, etc, etc. But it doesn't matter. The fact is that the Bond films have knit together various ingredients (which individually other films may possess more stylistically) in a highly successful and commercial manner. Audiences respond with genuine gusto to the films. In all likelihood Saltzman and Broccoli were lucky in hitting a formula just at the right moment.'

4

THE FILM STAR:
A BOND APART

4

The Film Star: A Bond Apart

*Not content to rest comfortably on his laurels as the suavest of
secret agents, he has continually sought challenges of the highest
order in his career and, in triumphantly surmounting them, has
created an extraordinary range of compelling characters to
delight audiences around the world and add further lustre to his
chosen medium.*

Sir Richard Attenborough CBE

Even before the Bond films were being shot, Connery had
become involved in a film which was both a critical and a
box-office success. This was *The Longest Day*, released just four
days after *Dr No*. It was based on a book by Cornelius Ryan
about the D-Day landings, produced by veteran American film
tycoon Darryl F. Zanuck, and reputed at the time to be the
most expensive black and white movie ever made. The film
looked at the 24 hours following the D-Day landings in France
by the Allied forces from the points of view of the British,
American, French and the Germans. Connery played an Irishman, Private Flanagan, and his appearance was unbilled, but
the cast read like a directory of film 'greats' and included John
Wayne, Robert Mitchum, Henry Fonda, Richard Burton, Kenneth More and Peter Lawford.

His first non-Bond film made under the terms of his contract
with Eon Productions was *Woman of Straw*, shot at Pinewood
studios with a relatively small cast. Here Connery played
Anthony Richmond, the nephew of Charles Richmond (Ralph
Richardson), a rich invalid looked after by a nurse, Maria,
played by Gina Lollobrigida. Connery read the script while he

was filming *From Russia with Love*, but did not have time to pay it the attention it deserved. In the film Anthony persuades Maria to marry the uncle on the basis that when he dies she will inherit the money and they will share it between them. The uncle dies unexpectedly and Maria is convicted of his murder, but it turns out that Anthony has been responsible for this and has framed Maria so that he will obtain all of the money for himself.

By the time filming was finished, Connery knew the film was not going to be a great success and he blamed himself for not having read the script properly before he had agreed to taking part. 'I won't make that mistake again,' he vowed. He developed a great admiration for Ralph Richardson and was later to say: 'An audience is never safe with him: you don't know what he's going to do next.'

The problems of typecasting quickly became evident despite the film's moderate success. According to *Variety*: '. . . Connery wanders around with the air of a man who can't wait to get back to being James Bond again.' The same comparison was drawn, albeit with a more complimentary slant, two years later, in 1966, when Connery starred in the Hollywood production *A Fine Madness* along with Joanne Woodward. 'Director Irvin Kershner has drawn effective performances from Connery,' said the *Variety* reviewer, 'who makes a good comic Kook in a switch from the somnabulism of his Bond roles.'

Woman of Straw was quickly followed by *Marnie*, a Hitchcock psycho-drama. It was based on a book of the same name written by the English novelist Winston Graham and published in 1961. Before signing Connery up for *Marnie*, Hitchcock tried to sign him to do two or three pictures. Beset already by problems of typecasting, Connery refused to commit himself to doing more than one film. And much to Hitchcock's surprise, he asked to see a copy of the script before committing himself, 'something which even great actors did not insist on,' according to a close Hitchcock aide.

Marnie is about a compulsive thief who steals from her employers, changing her identity and her job as soon as she has completed a robbery. New England businessman Mark Rutland (the role Hitchcock offered to Connery) nevertheless takes her on as a bookkeeper in view of his sexual fascination with her compulsion to steal.

Hitchcock had originally planned to give the title role to Grace Kelly and she had agreed to come out of 'retirement' to do the film, following her marriage to Prince Rainier of Monaco in 1956. Unfortunately she was forced to withdraw at the last moment because of her subjects' potential displeasure at seeing the wife of their head of state playing a compulsive thief. Hitchcock then cast Tippi Hedren, a former television model whom he had first used as leading lady in his previous film *The Birds*, as Marnie, and shooting began.

Hitchcock was legendary for his lack of interest in the actual shooting process. As James Mason has observed: 'He gets most fun out of making pictures at the blueprint stage: shooting is boring. He turns his back on the scene while they're shooting to prove this is something that happens automatically.' This approach pleased Connery, who was later to remark on how much he had enjoyed working with Hitchcock: 'I thought he was terrific. We got on famously. He was not one for giving great stage directions. His argument was that he was paying you enough so you should know what you were doing. Apart from that he was a terrific chap – funny, good-natured, erudite.'

According to Hitchcock's various biographers, the director gave Connery only two stage directions. One concerned Connery's tendency to let his mouth fall open when other characters were talking to him: 'I don't think people are interested in your dental work,' the old man told him. Hitchcock also advised Connery to 'sneak in some dog's feet', in other words to slow down his delivery of some of the lines.

Marnie was released amid a welter of half-hearted notices comparing it unfavourably to Hitchcock's previous pictures *Psycho* (1960) and *The Birds* (1963). Hitchcock himself was ambivalent about the film. He saw it as failing to portray, as the book had done, the inherent fetishism of a man who wanted to 'possess' a woman sexually simply because she was a thief. Some men like fat women, he reasoned, some like thin ones. Mark liked Marnie simply because she was a thief.

According to François Truffaut in his book *Hitchcock, The Definitive Study*, Hitchcock worried particularly about whether he had miscast Connery, with his unmistakable and only partly disguised Scottish accent, in the role of a New England businessman: 'I wasn't convinced that Sean Connery was a Philadelphia gentleman . . . In a story of this kind you need a real gentleman.'

Connery went on to play Joe Roberts in *The Hill*. This black and white film, made at MGM's British studios at Elstree and on location in Almeria, Spain, was directed by the American Sidney Lumet. It was set in a military detention camp in North Africa during the Second World War. The title refers to a rock and sand hill which the rebellious prisoners were forced to run up and down as a punishment by the sadistic Staff Sergeant Williams, played by Ian Hendry.

Connery enjoyed working with Lumet. He found the American director efficient and professional. Everything was done on time and within the constraints of the budget, and Connery was later to name *The Hill* as one of the movies from which he had derived most satisfaction 'because what one had set out to do, one more or less accomplished. [It was] directed by Sidney Lumet and I respect him because he's realistic and artistic. And . . . we finished a week under the production schedule. It was the professional approach. Even before being shown, *The Hill* had succeeded for me because I was . . . fully involved in the making of it.' Lumet was equally pleased with Connery. He had paid him $400,000 to play the part of Joe Roberts (virtually as much as the rest of the cast would earn from the film) because he could see that the big Scotsman's talents were being underused in the Bond films: 'When people saw Sean doing Bond,' says Lumet, 'they thought that was just flip easy stuff, but that's one of the hardest kinds of acting; only a real actor can do that. Cary Grant . . . would have been a wonderful dramatic actor and I'd always felt that about Sean. God knows, after *The Hill* I felt there was almost no telling where he would go.' The film was a critical success. It was chosen as the official British entry at the Cannes Film Festival and the reviewers were enthusiastic. According to *Variety*, Connery gave 'an intelligently restrained study, carefully avoiding forced histrionics'.

*

Once the Bond era was finally over, one of the main tasks lying before the disgruntled Sean Connery was to build a career as a versatile film actor, a career that could convince the world that he was more than just a secret agent, and that one of the publicity slogans that had promoted *Goldfinger* – 'Sean Connery *is* James Bond' – would no longer be appropriate. His other ambition was to gain further critical success, to be recognized by others in his own profession as the talented actor he felt he truly was.

Connery was also drawn to roles in adventure movies, not dissimilar to those he had watched as a boy in the Regal, the Caley and the New Coliseum, roles in which the hero was tough and macho, untouched by finer feelings, untainted by human vulnerability. One such film was *Shalako*, a British 'Western' in which Connery starred along with the glamorous Brigitte Bardot, Peter Van Eyck, Stephen Boyd, Honor Black-man and Jack Hawkins. The film is about a group of European aristocrats who go on a hunting expedition in New Mexico in the 1880s. Shalako is their guide.

The producer, a young Englishman by the name of Euan Lloyd, had originally wanted to cast Henry Fonda in the title role with Austrian actress Senta Berger playing the female lead. But having failed to raise the necessary finance, he approached Sean Connery who had just announced his retirement from the Bond role. Having read the script he agreed to play the part of Shalako which left Lloyd to find a female lead. On an off chance he sent the script to Brigitte Bardot in San Tropez. She liked the part she was offered, that of Countess Irina Lazaar, and Lloyd phoned Connery in the middle of the night to tell him the news.

'Bloody marvellous,' was Connery's reply, though whether he was being enthusiastic or sarcastic has never been recorded.

The problem for Lloyd was that Bardot had refused to com-mit herself until she had met her leading man. Anticipating possible ego problems if he asked Connery to go out to San Tropez for Bardot's approval, he arranged a meeting between the pair at Deauville. They got on well and contracts were subsequently signed.

Shalako was an adaptation of the book of the same name by English novelist Louis L'Amour, which had been published in

1962. It told the story of a former US army officer guiding a party of European aristocrats through Apache Indian territory while on safari in New Mexico in the 1880s. 'Women loved him, gunmen feared him,' ran the publicity blurb to the book. 'Apaches hated him – he stood between them and their prey.' Like *The Hill*, it was to be shot in Almeria, and Connery, travelling light as usual, arrived in the dusty Spanish city before Bardot to take lessons in horse-riding. He was worried about Bardot as the leading lady, concerned that she would be temperamental, difficult to work with, more concerned about self-publicity than putting in a good performance. She arrived, together with her entourage of minders, publicity co-ordinators and journalists, which had him shaking his head and making comments under his breath about her 'bloody circus'.

According to American gossip columnist Sheilah Graham, in her book *Scratch an Actor*, the two 'acted like two hounds on heat when they met, before the film started, to take photographs for publicity. If this was acting, they should both win an Oscar. Sean was panting after her, straddling over her on a bed, at the same time taking pictures of her while she lay back breathing seductively on the pillows while professional photographers recorded the scene.' Later, Bardot herself was to praise Connery for the support he had given her during shooting. As a leading lady she had long been used to taking responsibility for encouraging and advising less experienced actors and actresses. But for *Shalako* Connery took this role. '*Shalako* is Sean's film,' she was to say later. 'He carried all the weight on his shoulders.'

The film opened in London in September 1968 and the reviews were good. This pleased Connery immensely according to an article at the time in the *Scottish Sunday Express*: 'I own a large piece of it,' he said. 'Besides backing it, I took a deferred salary. It's a gamble, of course. But you've got to take a chance.'

Generally, the late sixties and early seventies were a highly active time for Connery. Some things happened; some were made to happen. He gave up smoking. He was awarded undisclosed libel damages in 1969 when he sued *France Soir* for its assertion, quite erroneous, that Broccoli and Saltzman had dispensed with his services because he was no longer fit to play the part. He acquired a number of company direc- torships. One of these was in Fernbroad Ltd., a property investment company. Another was in the Dunbar Bank, a Pall Mall merchant bank of which he and fellow golfing partner Iain Stewart were both directors, and which merged a few years later into Allied Dunbar, leaving himself and Stewart handsomely better off.

Additionally, his renunciation of all further involvement in the Bond roles had released him to pursue many of the interests he had never had time for. These branched out in a number of directions. One was television; here he became involved in a number of notable productions. The first was a documentary by Scottish Television, *Fairfields – Keel of Industry*, which was part of the 'Present Grandeur' series for which Connery did the voice-over. This charted the story of the Fair- fields shipyard in the Govan area of the Upper Clyde from the day it was announced that the yard's bankers, the Bank of Scotland, had foreclosed on it and the yard was going to close.

On 15 October 1965, the day the bankruptcy was announced, the yard had an order book worth £32 million and was, accord- ing to observers at the time, one of the most modern and best equipped shipyards in the UK. As a result of the outcry which followed the bankruptcy announcement, the UK government put up £1 million to keep it open while a consortium of promi- nent local businessmen, politicians and union leaders inves- tigated ways of keeping it open. The consortium was led by Iain Stewart who had been asked to take this on by his friend George Brown, the government minister who had sanctioned the loan. Stewart had directorships in a variety of major com- panies, including Scottish Television in Glasgow and the Dor- chester Hotel in London, and had been Captain of the Royal and Ancient, the oldest golf club in the world, at St Andrews. He was also Chairman of the family firm, Hall Thermotank Ltd, with offices just a stone's throw from the Govan shipyard and which did a lot of business in the vessels built on the Clyde. But he had no experience of shipyard techniques.

Despite the government's loan (at seven per cent interest),

Stewart reckoned that Fairfields would require a working capital of £2 million if it were to survive. Fortunately his friends Lord Thomson, Hugh Stenhouse and other wealthy Scottish businessmen enabled him to raise a further £650,000. He then took the audacious step of going round the 11 unions which were involved with the yard, persuading seven of them to put in £50,000 each. And on 22 December 1965 an announcement was made in the House of Commons that the money had been raised to save the yard by a unique combination of private capital, union funds and private grants. One of Stewart's first moves was to persuade Jim Houston, a business manager, to take on a senior management role. Houston had been brought up in the culture of American electronics and computer firms and was currently a director of Singers in Clydebank, then the largest manufacturing company in Scotland.

The second television production in which Connery was involved related closely to *Fairfields – Keel of Industry*. He contacted Iain Stewart to find out if the new ideas put forward in the programme might justify the making of a new documentary film, the current one having been filmed prior to the announcement that the yard was to be saved.

'Connery is a very nice man, a very modest man,' says Jim Houston, 'and he has a very strong social conscience. But he made a point which I think was very reasonable – he asked if this was all a load of codswallop or was there really anything in it.'

Stewart invited Connery to see for himself what was being achieved as a result of what was now known as the Fairfields Experiment. He spent time at the yard, talking to Stewart, Jim Houston and the shop stewards, talking to the men and women who worked there. The workers took to Connery from the start, recognizing the Scottish boy-made-good in the international film star and, as soon as they spoke to him, these street-wise men and women became aware of the fact that success had not turned his head. The admiration was mutual: Connery had a strong liking for the dry self-deprecatory humour of the yard's 'patter merchants'.

'They got very close with Sean and he got very close with them,' says Jim Houston. After a few days at the yard Connery knew there was a story to be told and that he could make a film of it. 'He has a very sharp mind, a very sharp mind indeed. He's a good businessman,' continues Houston.

'Iain Stewart called this an experiment,' says Houston. 'The point he was making was that it might fail – but if it succeeds it could be a pointer for the future. The yard was to be open to visits from anyone – even its competitors. Connery challenged Stewart, and Stewart immediately challenged him. And there was a friendship that grew up between Connery and Stewart – and between Connery and myself – which was very very strong.'

Connery and Stewart were an odd couple. Stewart was a 'boss's son', the type that the old Fountainbridge Connery would have shunned and despised. But despite the difference in their backgrounds, the two got on famously. Like Connery, Stewart had stayed close to his Scottish roots and they shared a passion for golf. 'I've seen Sean ribbing Iain about his better-class upbringing,' says Jim Houston. 'But I never ever saw friction between them.'

By the mid-sixties, then, the old Fountainbridge Connery had become the new Knightsbridge Connery – things had moved on. The Connery who had left Scotland over ten years before was now able to see his homeland with fresh eyes, to see the 'feudal atmosphere which still exists there', one which he thought was dragging the country down. When he accepted Iain Stewart's invitation to visit the yard, he discovered there an unusual *esprit de corps* which he believed was badly needed to bring Scotland back to her feet and he became very enthusiastic about what he found there.

Bill Hawkins was also involved in the Fairfields Experiment, having been seconded to Iain Stewart by Lord Thomson, a major shareholder in the new Fairfields. It was the first time he had met the actor. 'I think one of the most surprising things about him was his humility. I don't think he fully appreciated then just how successful he had been and what sort of international megastar he was.'

A few weeks after his initial meeting at the Fairfields yard, Connery was back there armed with a script written by Scots writer and actor Cliff Hanley, and accompanied by Brian Izzard, the flamboyant if overweight director who was immediately christened 'Miss Twiggy' by the Fairfields patter merchants. The documentary was to be financed jointly by Connery and Scottish Television and was to be entitled *The Bowler and the Bunnet*, the title a wry reference to the 'them 'n' us' class structure which pervaded in the shipyards. 'In those days if you were anything above foreman you wore a bowler hat,' says Bill Hawkins. The 'bunnets', worn by the workers, were a kind of reinforced flat cap generally made from tweed.

Connery spent several weeks at the yard, talking to workers, management, everyone involved in the design and construction of the great ships. 'He was interested in the way the shipyard workers had been treated,' says Hawkins. 'They really had been treated very very badly by the owners. When he came to Fairfields, he was crowded by a lot of people for the first few days and then he just settled in and became part of the scenery. I think they had established that he was an ordinary Scot. He was very much *for* the workers. He mixed with the trade union people in the evenings. He committed himself totally to the film-making. And he made it for nothing. He didn't take a fee.'

Connery and Izzard were very particular about the film. 'Everything had to be perfect,' says Houston, recalling how Connery, who had never before been in a shipyard, used to visit him on a daily basis during the making of the film to find out what was going on that day. 'It was all a series of wonders to him. He was very receptive to all kinds of ideas – some of which, incidentally, probably weren't very good ideas.' If it was interesting, the script had to be changed to accommodate it, to the extent that Cliff Hanley asked Jim Houston to limit the number of discussions he had with Connery.

When the film was complete, it was broadcast by only six stations on the ITV network, one of them Scottish Television. Billed as 'more than a study of an experiment in industrial relations, it is a frank appraisal of the attitudes of men who are traditional enemies – management and workers', the reviews were less than enthusiastic.

The *Glasgow Herald*, which had been opposed from the start to the setting up of the new Fairfields, did not review it at all. The *Scotsman* ran its review on a news page under the heading 'Showmanship spoils Clyde documentary'.

'While it succeeded in conveying the vigour and enthusiasm

of this revitalized yard,' it ran, 'it failed on the sociological level. More effort might have been made to explore the traditional mistrust of the bosses, or the attitude of the management to "the chaps down on the shop-floor". Everybody said his prepared piece, but there were few spontaneous shafts of insight. We were left with the vague impression of mutual suspicion remaining despite good intentions all round.'

The *Scotsman*'s sister paper, the *Evening News*, was much more complimentary. 'If *The Bowler and the Bunnet* proved anything other than that . . . Fairfields appear to be making a go of it on the Clyde, it was that Sean Connery has not been mooning around with his eyes shut while he's been doing the James Bond bit.

'Obviously, he has taken more than a passing interest in how good movies have been made, for his direction of this documentary . . . showed abundant touches of professionalism. For many viewers a programme about industrial relations could have been a crashing bore.

'The fact that it wasn't was due in the main to Connery, who presented an uncluttered picture of the shipbuilding scene at Govan from both sides of the fence.'

The Bowler and the Bunnet opens with scenes from a Scottish football match, and the observation, in Connery's rich drawl, that Scotland's most important export is people, the implication being that too many people have to leave the country in order to find work. It then cuts to Connery, casually dressed and wearing a bunnet, driving to Glasgow in his sports car. Once there he visits the Govan yard, talking to managers, Jim Houston among them, to shop stewards and workers, and explaining the nature of the experiment which is going on. At one point near the beginning of the film, Connery appears to cycle through a brick wall and into a derelict industrial building (they were not able to use the Fairfields premises because the shipyard was anything but derelict). To the tune of *Land of Hope and Glory* he cycles around on an old-fashioned grocer's bicycle while his voice-over tells us: 'To the workers' bitter eye the situation looks clear: the boss takes the gravy when the going is good and when things look bad he sells out, takes his money and vanishes. And that's the crux. The gulf is complete. The gulf between the bowler and the bunnet.' He talks of the yard being 'a kind of university', where people can be trained and retrained to master a variety of skills. He talks of the future of Scottish shipbuilding and manufacturing in general. And he talks about the prospect of nationalization of the shipyards, already being discussed by the Labour government of the day. 'If there is a merger of the Clyde shipyards,' he says, 'I myself think that the Fairfields plan is its biggest hope.'

Indeed, by 1967 the Fairfields Experiment was a proven success. The company had built five ships, delivered them all on time, and was making profits of £2.5 million in its third year.

Alas, this was not to continue. Just a few months after *The Bowler and the Bunnet* was broadcast, the Government announced its nationalization plans for the shipyards. Some five shipbuilding centres would be formed in the UK: Teeside, Tyneside, Northern Ireland, Lower Clyde and Upper Clyde. Fairfields was to become part of Upper Clyde Shipbuilders along with Yarrows, Browns, Connells and Stevens. Its uniqueness was to be lost: the experiment was to end. Stewart and Houston pleaded with the government that the Fairfields Experiment be preserved intact, but to no avail. Although Iain Stewart became Deputy Chairman of Upper Clyde, it was soon obvious to those involved that the unique structure of the revitalized Fairfields was to be lost and all the bad practices of the old yards were to be reinstated. As Bill Hawkins put it: 'We suddenly found that the shipyards were being run by the same old Families. It really screwed up Sean. He was livid about it.'

The management team responsible for launching the Fairfields Experiment soon became disillusioned and, one by one, left to become involved in a variety of other projects. Bill Hawkins left to join Granada Publishing but soon became disillusioned with that. This worked, however, to Connery's advantage. At a meeting with Iain Stewart at London's Dorchester Hotel, Bill Hawkins and Stewart discussed the viability of Hawkins setting up his own industrial public relations company, Industrial Communications Ltd. Sean Connery became a shareholder and director. 'Sean used to speak very sensibly and intelligently about PR matters,' says Hawkins. 'He was neither a journalist nor a PR man, just a very valuable person to have around. He knew a lot of people, showbiz people.'

During this time the films continued for Connery, though he desperately needed to make some which were more successful. *The Molly Maguires*, to be filmed in America, seemed to present just such an opportunity. It was the story of a group of striking Irish immigrant coal miners in Pennsylvania, and the subject-matter, coming hard on the heels of *The Bowler and the Bunnet*, was close to Connery's heart. He signed to play the leader of the striking miners along with Richard Harris, who was to play McPherson, a mole in the miner's camp. Samantha Eggar was signed as the leading lady.

Asked at the time why he was playing second billing to Richard Harris, he replied: 'They're paying me a million dollars for this picture. For that they can put a mule ahead of me.' By all accounts, he and Harris got on well during the filming. In his biography *Richard Harris*, Gus Smith records Harris as saying: 'After about ten days I had trouble with a scene. So I asked Sean what I was doing wrong and he helped me through. I think Sam (Samantha Eggar) was amazed to see two actors of our calibre helping each other, not trying to upstage each other.' *Time* magazine wrote: '. . . one of the screen's most underrated stars, an actor of tightly controlled power and technical accomplishment'.

Connery's association with the Fairfields Experiment was also to have unexpected benefits to his film career a couple of years later when he was working on *The Red Tent*, released in 1969. This was an Italian/Soviet co-production about polar explorer Roald Amundsen which was largely filmed in Russia. 'In those days,' says Connery, 'the Russians had serious reservations about the idea of James Bond coming to make a film in the Soviet Union. Of course, the Bond films had never been shown in cinemas there, but the embassies used to run them on 16mm. So I was very big on the embassy circuit, but no one in the street knew me from a bag of beans.' It was the discovery by the Soviet authorities that Connery had made *The Bowler and the Bunnet* that oiled the wheels of Soviet bureaucracy and allowed the film to proceed. 'They asked for a print of it and it's now in the Mosfilm archives. Once they'd seen it and found out about my tenement background they had no trouble accepting me,' he recalls.

Connery's last appearance as an actor in a television play was in *MacNeil*, the first of a trilogy of plays by Alun Owen, broadcast on 1 February 1969. Here he played a master carpenter, separated from his wife and supporting his 20-year-old daughter whose relationship with her father is put under severe stress by his father's weakness for women. *Variety*'s review included the comment that 'Connery plays an aged man very convincingly.'

In 1967 Connery also became involved in theatrical promotion, putting money up for Frank Hauser to move a production of Ben Jonson's *Volpone* from the Oxford Playhouse to the Garrick Theatre in London's West End where it ran for a six-week season. He also had a pecuniary interest in Gogol's *The Diary of a Madman* running at the Duchess Theatre for a month and directed by Irvin Kershner.

In 1969 he directed his first West End play *I've Seen You Cut Lemons* starring his wife Diane Cilento and Robert Hardy. This opened at the Fortune Theatre on 16 December 1969 but critical reviews were poor: 'Goodness knows why Sean Connery chose this psycho melodrama as his directorial debut,' said *Plays and Players* in February 1970, after the play had closed. 'He kept it going with a quiet desperation, but judgment had best be reserved until he shows his colours in a better vehicle.'

5

THE PHILANTHROPIST

5

The Philanthropist

*Sean has such high ideals. He is a totally genuine man. He is
always shocked by people.*

Micheline Roquebrune

The year 1970 appears to have been a quiet time for Connery.
His venture into theatrical directing was now over and
his latest film, *The Red Tent*, had already been released. The
only filming on the immediate horizon was for *The Anderson
Tapes*, a police thriller, directed by Sidney Lumet, his all-time
favourite film director. The story concerns an ex-convict, the
role Connery played, who plans an elaborate raid on a high-
class apartment building but fails to take into account the
closed-circuit television security cameras which are recording
his every move on the videotape from which the film derives its
name. The film was well received, the *Times* critic writing that
'. . . a laconic, balding Sean Connery is admirable.' Outside of
the film world, however, much was happening. Connery was
actively involved in the organization of a charity golf tournament, the Sean Connery Pro-Am, and in the setting up of a
new charity.

On the golf front, this was now being honed to something like
perfection and he was regularly getting round in less than
eighty. As a result, he won the men's prize at an international
charity golf tournament in Casablanca in 1970. The lady's prize
was taken by an attractive red-headed French artist now living in
North Africa, Micheline Roquebrune (Mrs Cosman). 'It was love
at first sight for the two of us,' Micheline was to say later. 'I was

married; he was married. His wife was in Spain and my husband was playing golf with the King of Morocco [but] when the prizegiving came we danced the whole night. For me he was the most exotic person I had met in my life.'

During 1971 Connery and Micheline met twice and by the end of that year he and Diane were officially separated. He told Micheline: 'I'm basically very serious and I don't want to play games with you.'

'That was really the beginning of what is now our life,' she says.

Since making *The Bowler and the Bunnet* in 1967, Connery, Sir Iain Stewart and Jim Houston had met frequently met at the Dorchester Hotel. 'Sean, Iain and I came to the conclusion that maybe there was something else we could do which was similar to Fairfields,' says Jim Houston. At subsequent meetings, both at the Dorchester and at 'Lochbrae', Sir Iain Stewart's home just outside Glasgow, they continued the conversation. 'We finished at Fairfields in 1968 and it would be in '69–'70 when we were carrying on these discussions. We met regularly and consolidated the idea in 1970. It took us the best part of a year and a bit. We invited people like Sir Samuel Curran, the great Glasgow lawyer John Tyndal, who was to be the architect of the constitution we were to set up, Alastair Dunnett, ex-editor of the *Scotsman*, and world champion motor racing driver Jackie Stewart.'

By the beginning of December 1970 a meeting was set up at the Gleneagles Hotel between all the interested parties (who later also included Connery's old art school buddy Richard Demarco, by then an internationally known art gallery owner in Edinburgh). The decision was taken to set up an educational charity which would fund projects in Scotland for the benefit of Scotland and which would also send young Scots abroad to learn skills they could not learn in their native land.

'Connery had made a lot of money,' says Bill Hawkins. 'He had made some very good deals. He wanted to help Scotland. He couldn't become involved in industry as such because he didn't know much about it, so he had this idea of helping young Scots – sports people, musicians and the like – on the basis that if they could contribute to Scotland afterwards, then we would help them.'

But it was Sir Iain Stewart who knew which buttons to push. 'Scotland was very much run by the establishment,' says Bill Hawkins. 'I think Sean saw an opening to help Scotland through the contacts Iain Stewart had. Iain knew more people in business, commerce and education in Scotland, whereas Sean's friends were mainly showbiz friends in England and America. The trustees were people of stature. Sean did not know these people as Iain did.'

The Trust, known as the Scottish International Education Trust (SIET), was formally established on 4 December 1970. The principal aims as outlined in its constitution were 'to promote individual Scottish talent among young people which will be seen to be supported in Scotland and will retain its roots and interests for the benefit of Scotland' and 'to support projects which seem to the Trustees especially valuable in contributing to the cultural, economic or social development of Scotland or the improvement of the Scottish environment'.

'There was never a fussy and loud inauguration of the SIET, because in the early days our income was very small,' says Jim Houston. 'It mainly came from pro-am golf tournaments and race meetings at Hamilton. The SIET has never had appeals to the public; all the money raised has been raised by the trustees themselves.'

One of its first public activities was to organize a dinner at the Central Hotel in Glasgow for the editors of all the Scottish newspapers with a view to explaining to them what the SIET was all about. 'In the early days of the Trust there were several people who really felt that it was some sort of cover-up for Sean Connery and his money,' says Jim Houston. And later, in 1974 when Connery decided to move away from Britain to become a tax exile in Spain, his opponents argued that it was hypocritical to encourage others to retain their 'roots and interests' in Scotland while living oneself in the Spanish sunshine.

Some of the early trustees, people like John Tyndal, Alastair Dunnett and Sir Iain Stewart himself, had already been heavily involved with charity work and the early fund-raising for SIET copied techniques they had used to raise money for the Saints and Sinners, another fund-raising organization in London. One of the early ventures was the Sean Connery Pro-Am Golf Tournament at Troon in July 1970. The prize-money was £15,000, at that time almost more than any previous prize-money outside the USA. According to the *Glasgow Herald*: 'in scale . . . nothing of its kind has been held in Britain.' Connery had 'used his persuasive powers to assemble a talented company of professionals' which included Tony Jacklin, Arnold Palmer, Gary Player, Billy Casper, Lee Trevino and local man Bernard Gallagher. They were to be 'teamed with amateur partners from the worlds of showbusiness, golf and other sports' including Stanley Baker, Bruce Forsyth, Harry Secombe (a late replacement for Bob Hope) and Australian tennis ace Rod Laver.

Film premières were another source of funds. Connery had just finished making *The Anderson Tapes* and wanted the UK première of the film to be held in Glasgow, with the proceeds going to charity. He approached the head of Columbia with this in mind, only to be told it was out of the question.

'Why?' he asked.

'Because we've never done a première in Scotland before,' came the reply.

'Well, that's as good a reason as any why we should do one now,' said Connery, and in the end Columbia agreed. Given the subject-matter of the film it was deemed appropriate that the proceeds be split between the SIET and a police charity.

By then, Houston was Chairman of the Trust and was struggling to balance the books. Each event would raise around £10–15,000 but that was scarcely enough to service the Trust. 'We really need more money,' Houston told the assembled trustees at one of their quarterly meetings held either in Edinburgh, Glasgow, St Andrews or London. 'If we had more money we could invest it, we could get things moving, because money makes money.' Connery consequently donated most of his fee, $1m (then worth £413,000), for *Diamonds Are Forever* to the SIET, tax-free. This was banked in the Dunbar Bank – of which both Connery and Stewart were directors – and then astutely invested so that the interest which accrued became the money which the Trust gave out in grants. 'That was when the Trust really arrived,' says Jim Houston. 'That money has grown and grown and we have spent and spent. And we are able with good management, and extremely low costs, to ensure that plenty of money is coming in which can be paid out. In addition we can see the capital increasing.'

At the time Connery himself was quoted in the *Evening News* as saying: 'The Scottish International Education Trust has been fermenting in my mind for a long time and that takes care of all my charitable gestures apart from my Variety Club golfing dates which will continue.'

By 1971 Richard Demarco had taken over the directorship of the Trust and Jackie Stewart and Sir Samuel Curran had joined the trustees. 'With a combination of these people you could get anything done,' says Bill Hawkins, who was himself appointed to handle the public relations needs of the charity. The offices of the SIET were located in an office on the top floor of the building occupied by Demarco's art gallery in Melville Crescent, Edinburgh.

Richard Demarco found his role very demanding. 'I was inundated with requests all over the place. I couldn't really do that job and run my gallery because my gallery was really a difficult thing to run and I did not have all the time and energy required. I realized it needed someone with total commitment.' Sir Norman Graham took over in 1972.

Generally, however, fund-raising events were few and far between following the *Diamonds Are Forever* donation. 'When someone starts a charity with half a million pounds, it's very difficult to ask people to help you,' says Houston.

Some of the other fund-raising activities which helped bolster the coffers of the SIET have included the European première of *Diamonds Are Forever*, held at the Odeon in Edinburgh in 1972. This was attended by Scottish personalities such as world champion boxer Ken Buchanan, world champion racing driver Jackie Stewart and football manager Tommy Docherty. The proceeds of £5,000 were split between the SIET and Edinburgh press charities.

'Since then, we've done quite a few world premières,' says Jim Houston. 'We did *A Bridge Too Far* in Minneapolis. That was Jackie Stewart's idea. He had a lot of contacts in Minneapolis through his racing and he knew a group of business people who did a lot of work for boys' clubs. We'd share the proceeds fifty-fifty with the boys' clubs.' These clubs had been founded by a group of local socially minded businessmen who saw them as a way of keeping boys off drugs, off the streets, out of trouble.

The party of SIET trustees who flew out from Britain to Minneapolis included Connery, Sir Iain Stewart, Houston, Jackie Stewart, Tyndal, David Yellowless and Sir Norman Graham. Each paid their own way. Jackie Stewart had organized the reception through his connections with Ford Motors and a convoy of Ford cars (painted tartan!) came to pick them up at the airport. Jackie Stewart's fame throughout America as both a racing driver and a commentator was evident when queues formed for autographs for himself and Connery: Jackie Stewart's queue was six or seven times longer than Connery's!

Even in its first 'year and a bit', when Richard Demarco was Executive Director, the SIET was to make grants to individuals with many different talents. 'We had every possible kind of request,' says Demarco, 'from ice skating to academic study – and every now and again art. I remember making it possible for the famous artist, Will Maclean, to be given £3,000. That enabled him to pack up teaching for six months and get down to being the artist he really was. And what enabled me to pass the thing through the committee was the fact that he was from the Isle of Skye, from a great fishing tradition and he was making a study of the dying herring fisheries in the Minch.'

Since then, the SIET has supported many projects, some of them suggested by its trustees and friends. Many of the grants went to young people whom the trustees perceived to be of outstanding ability, people like Edinburgh jazz saxophonist Tommy Smith, whom the Trust sent to Chicago. Other grants have gone to universities and national sports bodies. Still others have gone to the National Youth Orchestra of Scotland, the Scottish Chamber Orchestra, Scottish Opera and to Scottish conservationist projects.

Not all of Connery's philanthropic ideas met with such untrammelled success. Some fell on stony ground, on very stony ground indeed. One of these was his plan, announced in 1970, to raise money to help renovate the Scottish national football stadium, Hampden Park, which for years had been falling into disrepair. Connery, still passionately interested in football, desperately wanted to help. His plan was to organize a football match between a Rangers-Celtic select and the Brazilian national side, then world champions. He estimated that it would generate as much as £80,000 and he offered personally to underwrite it to the tune of £30,000. The plan fell through after Connery flew into Glasgow for talks with Willie Allen, then secretary of the Scottish Football Association, the governing body of football in Scotland. Allen turned Connery down flat, accusing him of trying to 'organize football' in Scotland which, under their rules, only they were allowed to do.

In a letter to the *Scottish Daily Express*, Connery explained his position: 'My idea was to invite Brazil, World Cup winners, to compete for the Glasgow Charities Cup (which had died a few years earlier from lack of support) against a Rangers and Celtic select at Hampden Park. The financial take would have been approximately £80,000 to be divided between Glasgow Charities, Queens Park and the Scottish International Education Trust.

'I was prepared to underwrite the scheme myself with £30,000.

'BUA Caledonian had offered their support to the tune of 22 air tickets for the Brazilians and a junket flight from London to bring up representatives from all the embassies.

'I presented all the above mentioned to Mr W. Allen of the SFA, who is also on the board of the Glasgow Charities.

'At no time in our conversation did I want to "organize football", as he is quoted as saying, and I take great exception to this remark. As Mr Allen must recall, I pressed for him to run the whole show as I was not in a position to do so.

'I am completely in favour of the professional approach to all things which, in turn, explains my reactions to the "Save Hampden" campaign.'

In 1971 Connery exploited his need for critical acclaim by 'setting up' his own production company, Tantallon Films (or, more accurately, taking it over, it originally having been set up in 1968 by someone else) as part of the agreement between United Artists and himself. His agent Richard Hatton and producer Denis O'Dell were fellow directors of the company. In Connery's words: 'I'm setting up my own company. I'll have a meeting soon with my accountant, agent and lawyer to determine the name of it. We want to get key management. One of the problems in the industry is that too many of the administrative people don't know anything about picture making.

'Already I've got my producer, Denis O'Dell, a good man who started as a tea boy and worked his way up and he's done the lot. He's highly respected by the major companies. He produced *The Magic Christian* and worked with Dick Lester in the Beatles' films.

'We expect to sign a dependable financial man who's come through the ranks, plus a first-class secretary. We'll want an advisory committee to keep the whole operation professional and flexible . . . a tight unit which is really what Upper Clyde Shipbuilders should have been.

'My company will be making at least two pictures for United Artists and in the first of these, my acting role is too long and involved for me to direct as well and I'd rather leave the acting/directing experiment to the next one.'

The first Tantallon film, *The Offence*, was to be an adaptation of a John Hopkins stage play called *This Story of Yours* and was to be directed by Sidney Lumet. 'We'll make it for under a million dollars because Sidney is that kind of efficient director,' Connery is reported as saying at the time. 'Both films I did with him came in under schedule. The kind of films I want to make will mean that the people who make the most sacrifices will make the most money. Like me and the director.'

In this film, a psychological drama made under the running title *Something Like the Trust*, Connery plays a tough cop, Detective Sergeant Johnson, investigating the rape of a schoolgirl. During interrogation he beats the suspect Kenneth Baxter (Ian Bannen) so violently that the man dies. According to the business prediction in *Cinema T.V. Today*, the film would be 'good to very good in carefully selected cinemas and art houses, otherwise variable'. Even before it was made, United Artists had been distinctly uneasy about it. The box-office potential, they said, was poor – and they were right. It took years before the film showed a profit.

At the time of setting up Tantallon, the second film – which Connery was both to act in *and* direct – had not been chosen, though he was working on a film script for Shakespeare's

Macbeth commenced way back in Spain while Diane was working on *Hybrid*, her second novel. 'But I'm hanging on to it until I see what Polanski's version is like.' In the event, a second film was never made.

Zardoz was filmed after the launch of *The Offence*. Box office receipts were poor and reviews were mixed, the *New Yorker* describing it as a 'gloriously fatuous' film.

Connery went on to film *Ransom*, which again was poorly received. He then teamed up again with Sidney Lumet to appear as the grave Colonel Arbuthnot in the film adaptation of Agatha Christie's *Murder on the Orient Express*. While the film was a hit, its success was diluted for Connery by the number of major international stars within the cast. Connery had only seventh billing after Albert Finney, Lauren Bacall, Martin Balsam, Ingrid Bergman, Jacqueline Bisset and Jean-Pierre Cassel.

Although the early seventies were a happy time for Connery, something happened which was to spoil his pleasure. His father, who had never been ill in his life, died of cancer. This affected him deeply: it stopped him in his tracks and slowed down his progress towards other goals.

There were also other developments in his personal, and professional, life. By 1973 Connery and Diane Cilento had been separated for two years and divorce proceedings were now in train. The hearing at which the divorce petition was finally granted took place at a divorce court in London in October 1973, presided over by Judge Braithwaite. Connery arrived for the court case dressed, for once, immaculately. Gone were the casual clothes; back was the smart-suited Connery of the Bond films. During the hearing, his Counsel, Jeremy Tatham, said that both parties wished for a 'civilized end' to their marriage. Cilento was given custody of the children and Connery 'reasonable access' to them. In return, Connery was to provide two capital sums: the first was to go to Diane 'in full and final settlement' of her claims against him. The second would form a trust fund for Giovanna and Jason, the capital eventually going to Jason. The sums were never disclosed but were substantial amounts. Kenneth Passingham, author of a biography on Connery, was sued for libel by the actor for suggesting, incorrectly, that the actor had not made sufficient provision for his divorced wife.

Outside the courtroom, the reporters were waiting to pounce. They already knew something of his relationship with Micheline Roquebrune and wanted to know if he had plans to remarry. Connery was curt: he felt his fingers had been burned by speaking too openly to the press in the past. He told them: 'I am making no comment on my private life from this day on, whether it is about marriage or marrying – something I have tried to do in the past without much success.'

By the mid-seventies the UK film industry was in terminal decline. The growth of television had attacked cinema attendance figures particularly badly in the UK and the studios were cutting back. Increasingly, major British film stars were having to turn to Hollywood for suitable roles. Additionally, Britain's election of a new Labour government in 1974 was expected to squeeze the rich. Film stars were beginning to leave the UK to set up residence in countries where they would not be exposed to what they saw as 'punitive' tax regimes. As indicated earlier, Connery decided to join them. 'I didn't take a long time to think about it,' he was to say later. 'It really was a series of events – the 98 per cent tax I was paying and the possibility of making three films outside the UK which meant that I was not going to be here for 36 weeks of the year.' He became resident in The Bahamas, bought a villa in Marbella, Spain, close to where he and Diane Cilento had shared their smallholding with Sir Iain Stewart, and he and Micheline moved in together.

Those three films, *Robin and Marian*, *The Wind and the Lion* and *The Man Who Would Be King*, marked something of a peak in Connery's career. In *Robin and Marian*, released in 1976, Connery plays an ageing Robin Hood with Audrey Hepburn as 'Maid' Marian, in a cast which included such well-known names as Robert Shaw, Richard Harris and Denholm Elliott. Connery himself was pleased with the film according to Richard Demarco. It was popular too at the box-office and with most, if not all, of the critics. *Films and Filming* spoke of: 'Sean Connery's thoughtful interpretation . . .' whereas *Variety* wrote of 'a disappointing and embarrassing film; disappointing because Sean Connery, Audrey Hepburn and the brilliant Robert Shaw and a screenplay by Jack Goldman ought to add up to something even in the face of Richard Lester's flat direction; embarrassing because the incompatible blend of tongue-in-cheek comedy, adventure and romance gives the Robin Hood-revisited film the grace and energy of a geriatrics' discothèque.'

The Wind and the Lion was a Hollywood movie filmed largely on location in Almeria, released in the UK in October 1975, directed and written by John Milius; it also starred actor/director John Huston. Connery was playing the part of a Berber chieftain opposite leading lady Candice Bergen. As with many of Connery's films, reviews were a mixed bag. According to Leslie Halliwell, the film was 'confused and unexciting', but *Variety* reckoned Connery had scored 'one of his major screen impressions'.

Leading lady Candice Bergen was equally impressed. In her well-written autobiography *Knock Knock*, she said: 'While signing a Scot to play a legendary Berber chieftain seemed to some a quirky piece of casting, Sean gave an effortless performance: strong and dashing, witty and wry. He has that same wryness in life – a laconic sense of humour, an easy sense of fun. But what struck me as most unusual in a star of his stature was his lack of vanity, his comfortable sense of assurance. There was an honesty and directness about Sean, a wholeness, a manliness, that stardom has not eroded.'

Perhaps the non-Bond role he is best known for is his performance as Daniel Dravot with long-time friend Michael Caine in the film version of the Rudyard Kipling short story *The Man Who Would Be King*.

Veteran film director John Huston had been 'toying with the idea' of making a film based on the Kipling story for 20 years or more. In the late fifties he had just signed up Humphrey Bogart and Clark Gable to play the lead role when Bogart fell ill and died. The idea was temporarily shelved. In 1960, after directing *The Misfits* with Gable in the leading role, he decided to try again and set about the task of casting Bogart's role. But Gable died and the idea was once again shelved.

It was not until 1973 that, at the behest of producer John Foreman, the idea was taken out again, dusted down and the script sent to Paul Newman for consideration. Newman was initially enthusiastic about the project but on further consideration decided that the leading roles would be better played by Englishmen. 'For Christ's sake, John,' he is reported to have said. 'Get Connery and Caine.'

The film tells the story, almost entirely in flashback, of two former British Army sergeants: Daniel Dravot (played by Sean Connery) and Peachy Carnehan (Michael Caine), now organizing a gun-running and smuggling racket, who decide to set themselves up as kings in Kafiristan, a country closed to foreigners. The film was shot in 14 weeks in 1975, entirely around Marrakesh in Northern Africa, an area much used for film sets which require semi-desert conditions.

Like Hitchcock, Huston gave the actors freedom to use their own talents to the full. His most important stage direction came in the form of a briefing to the actors before filming began. 'Huston said that the two men in Kipling's short story were really two sides of the same man and that was how we should play it,' Connery was to say later. 'After that, Huston didn't do very much at all, which suited me, because I like to go off on the set and dream up all kinds of things.'

Caine recalls that the cast was put up in the Manoumia, one of the best hotels in Marrakesh. Huston had flown over from Mexico, where he was living, bringing with him his assistant and collaborator Gladys Hill. One of his first announcements to them was that he had dropped Tessa Dahl, daughter of author Roald Dahl, for the part of Princess Roxanne. She was too white, he said, to play an Indian princess. Who could he find at such short notice to play the part? All eyes turned on Shakira Caine, Michael's Indian wife and, after some resistance, she eventually agreed to play the part.

In his autobiography, Caine tells an interesting story about the shooting of the film. Connery persuaded Caine to go to the local 'disco' which turned out to be little more than a café in which records were played. Being a Muslim country, women were not allowed into the 'disco', so there were only men there when they arrived with their drivers. Also, soft drinks only were available because alcohol went against the teachings of the Koran. According to Caine, Connery was so keen on dancing that he ended up dancing with Caine's driver, the better-looking of the two.

It was during the filming that Connery announced to the cast that he had secretly married Micheline Roquebrune some months earlier on Gibraltar. News of the wedding had been carried in *The Times* the day after it took place, but it had not been widely reported.

The film tested Connery's determination to do as many as possible of his own stunts. As long ago as the *Playboy* interview of 1965, he had been telling journalists: 'There *are* doubles, but I usually do my own stunts.' Towards the end of the film, Daniel Dravot is executed by being made to stand in the centre of a rope bridge over a deep ravine while the ropes are ceremonially cut. The bridge used for shooting had been made by local people and appeared to Connery to be unstable, and he hesitated before taking his courage in his hands and walking out to the centre. There he sang, as he was required to, while a priest cut false ropes. Then, and only then, was his place taken by a stunt man who did the actual fall.

This was the film Connery was later to say was the one for which he *should* have won an Oscar. Caine too was enthusiastic. 'I think *The Man Who Would Be King* is one of the finest films in which I have ever appeared and one that I think will last long after I am gone,' he said. 'I think I'm right in saying the camera picked up how well Sean and I worked together. That was easy for us because we were already into that relationship. The warmth between us was there. Working with Sean was a real pleasure. I had rarely worked with an actor who was so unselfish and generous, so much so that you could experiment and take chances and not expect to find a knife in your back if it went wrong.'

But reviews were mixed. According to *Variety*, 'Connery, in the title role, gives a generally credible, but not very sympathetic, portrayal of the man thrust into potential greatness . . .' while *Films and Filming* wrote: 'Dravot calls for intricacies of characterization and obtains them from Sean Connery, good as he has ever been and perhaps at his very best . . .'

Another problem for both Connery and Caine was that when they totted up what they had earned from the film and compared it with the balance sheet of the distributors, Allied Artists, there was a discrepancy. Connery had negotiated a good deal for them of $250,000 plus five per cent of the gross. Connery and Caine jointly took Allied Artists to court for the underpayment of just over $100,000 each, Connery saying that they had only paid him enough for *The Man Who Would Be Prince*. Allied Artists retaliated by countersuing them for conspiring to damage the company by publishing false and defamatory statements. As the case went on, it became clear that if Connery and Caine were to win, it would be a minimal loss to Allied Artists. If, however, Allied Artists were to win, Connery and Caine would be bankrupt. And though they must both have been deeply worried about the potential outcome, they stuck to their guns and Allied paid up.

During the following year, 1976, Connery was offered the part of Major General Roy Urquhart in *A Bridge Too Far*, a Second World War epic to be directed by Richard Attenborough. Like *The Longest Day*, this was based on a novel of the same name by Cornelius Ryan. It tells the story of Operation Market Garden, a disaster at Arnhem in Holland which resulted in many unnecessary Allied casualties.

When Connery was first approached, he was unsure whether or not to do the film, which was about a very emotional and sensitive subject. Eventually he agreed and once he had done so, it persuaded others to sign too. As with *The Longest Day*, the eventual cast included a host of established stars – Dirk Bogarde, James Caan, Michael Caine, Elliott Gould, Anthony Hopkins and Robert Redford – and the budget was $25 million.

The location filming of the Dutch scenes had a big effect on Connery: 'It wasn't till I saw the cemeteries that I really understood the waste of war. Rows and rows and rows of them. Killed when hardly more than boys. The graveyards are beautifully kept. Each grave is looked after by one of the local schoolchildren who passes on the responsibility when he or she leaves school.'

Although the film had been financed by Hollywood and was well received outside the United States, American critics did not take it seriously. Nevertheless, the public disagreed and it was a box-office success on both sides of the Atlantic. In the

UK, it won eight BAFTA nominations and four awards, but in the States it was not nominated for a single Oscar.

A Bridge Too Far was followed by *Meteor*, a disaster both with the critics and at the box office. This was followed by a British film, *The First Great Train Robbery*, which told the story of a crook (played by Connery) who, in the last part of the nineteenth century, hatched a plot to steal gold being shipped to pay UK troops in the Guinea. The film, and Connery's performance in it, received glowing tributes in the critical press but was quickly followed by another of Connery's filmic 'mistakes' (of which he made a good many), *Cuba*. Much of it was filmed close to his home in southern Spain but he was deeply disappointed with the final cut and shut himself up in Marbella to lick his wounds.

The founding of the Scottish International Education Trust in 1970 did not put an end to Connery's other charitable contributions nor were they confined to Scottish causes. In 1980 he came to the rescue of the National Youth Theatre (NYT) in London with a gift of £50,000, although he had no connection with the theatre and had never acted with it. He gave the money because the NYT was in danger of going out of business. 'British actors and actresses, writers and directors,' said Connery, 'are among the best in the world. We come second to no one. The NYT is one source of this talent, a source that everyone should be proud of. It shouldn't have to go cap in hand for money.'

6

THE NATIVE RETURNS

6

The Native Returns

Not since . . . I directed Gary Cooper in High Noon *had I come across a man like Sean, not only a great natural actor, but a hell of a man.*

Fred Zinnemann

In the mid-seventies, Kevin McClory, who had been made a millionaire several times over by his income from *Thunderball*, began to conceive a remake of the film. He gave it the provisional title *James Bond of the Secret Service* and it was subsequently renamed *Warhead*. He started working on scripts for the production but after several set-backs, mainly legal battles with Eon Productions which claimed an interest in the story, he lost interest in the idea. He sold those scripts he had developed together with the rights to any future films to American film producer Jack Schwartzman.

Connery had been involved in the development of one of the scripts and in 1981 Schwartzman approached him to take on the role again, almost 20 years since he had first been approached by Broccoli and Saltzman to play Bond in *Dr No*. He was interested. It was ten years since he had last done a Bond film (*Diamonds Are Forever*) and the bad memories had faded. The films he had made since his successful adventure trilogy in the mid-seventies (*Robin and Marian*, *The Wind and the Lion* and *The Man Who Would Be King*) – films like *Meteor*, *Cuba*, *Outland*, *Time Bandits*, *The Man with the Deadly Lens* – had not done particularly well at the box-office or with the critics. Some, in fact, had been unmitigated disasters. *Outland* was a space-age thriller directed by Peter Hyams with a *High Noon* story-line. In *Time Bandits*, directed by the *Monty Python* animator Terry Gilliam, which tells the story of a boy's journey through time, Connery had agreed to play the part of Agamemnon on the basis that his name was a lure for other actors: 'The problem was that they couldn't get the film off the ground, so if I did Agamemnon then they would get the other actors.' Filming of *The Man with the Deadly Lens* followed hard on the heels of what Connery saw as his success in *Outland* and he took to it with enthusiasm, playing the part of a journalist on the track of infamous goings-on.

In respect of the Schwartzman offer, he took advice from those closest to him, particularly from his wife Micheline: 'Why not?' she said. 'What would you risk? After all these years it might be interesting.'

'She encouraged me – virtually challenged me – to do it,' he said. When he read the script he liked it immediately: 'It was romantic and pre-empted all the bullshit I knew would be written about my coming back to Bond.'

In addition to the Connerys' house near Nassau and the villa in Spain, they had a flat in Los Angeles. Connery's relationship with Micheline was much calmer and less turbulent than that with Diane Cilento, partly because they did not have the conflicting demands of acting lives. Where his life with Diane had been plagued by practical problems such as her whereabouts when he was filming, his whereabouts when she was filming and responsibility for looking after the children, Micheline was able to be flexible enough to spend time with Connery while filming and to look after Jason and her son Stefan when they were home from school. 'She's very much for what I want to do, where I want to go,' Connery was to say later. Micheline was there when he needed her, a more conventional wife and home-maker than Diane had ever been: 'She really made this whole place in Spain what it is.'

Jason was to tell a *Sunday Times* journalist many years later that 'my stepmother was marvellous at bringing us together as a family with her son Stefan.'

For his part, Connery was anything but a conventional husband. 'He is not the orthodox normal husband,' said Micheline. 'He is very much a loner. He needs me, but he also needs his privacy.'

The film, *Never Say Never Again*, a title suggested by Micheline, was to be produced by Kevin McClory and Jack Schwartzman and to be directed by Irvin Kershner, with whom Connery had already worked on *A Fine Madness* way back in the sixties. Orson Welles had originally been signed to play arch-villain Blofeld and Edward Fox to play Bond's boss 'M'. Connery was to collaborate on the script with McClory and writer Len Deighton and to have casting approval. The film was to be made on location in The Bahamas and Okinawa, Japan but as a result of legal problems relating to film rights, it was to be three years before it was finally shot.

On its release it was a box-office success, though Micheline was reportedly upset when she saw Connery's lingering screen kiss with leading lady Barbara Carrera. By the end of 1983 the film had taken over $51 million in the States and had broken box-office records in Italy, Holland, France and Switzerland. Even the hard-to-please Connery was satisfied with the finished product, if not by the way it came to be put together. 'My main concern was whether I could do it as well being 13 years older. I've not necessarily tried to play Bond as an older man. Nor do I feel that one should attach any major importance to age.'

But it had taken four years from start to finish, and for a man who valued professionalism and efficiency, this was not acceptable. 'I hadn't anticipated the production problems. I've been involved in it for two years . . . including the filming and the pre- and post-production.

'I suppose its basic ingredients are an awful lot of in-fighting and a great deal of money lavished on it. Personally I think it could be ten per cent better, but show me the film that works out entirely the way it was conceived.

'I think this is the best Bond; for the casting Edward Fox has the role of "M" for example. He's exactly right as the clinical computerized Englishman. We have to believe Bond has moved with the times and Edward was a first choice to contrast with the grey-type character Fleming created played by old Bernie (Bernard Lee).

'We had to work on *Never Say* within the framework and limitations we were allowed. United Artists and Cubby Broccoli spent that last 18 months and $2 million fighting us and that was quite stupid because they lost every round. Broccoli has 18 per cent of *Never Say* by the way so I don't know what he's complaining about.'

After filming *Never Say Never Again*, Connery, who had averaged two to three films annually since 1961, was not to work to any large extent for four years. The only other films he made were *The Sword of the Valiant*, poorly received and lost amidst the publicity surrounding *Never Say Never Again*, and *Five Days One Summer*, directed by Fred Zinnemann. Here he played a middle-aged married doctor who goes on holiday to the Alps with a girl 25 years younger. This reduction in his work rate was due partly to the production difficulties he had experienced in the making of *Never Say Never Again*. He blamed Jack Schwartzman. 'I wouldn't touch Jack Schwartzman with the proverbial barge-pole,' he said once the dust had settled on the production. 'You salvage it as best you can. But yes, the hassles did leave me disillusioned with the industry for a while. I even considered writing a little book on it. But then I thought, why stir up all the aggravation again. It's probably better left alone.'

In larger part, his period of self-imposed virtual 'unemployment' was a result of bad news he had received from his brother Neil at the beginning of the summer of 1981. His mother, Euphamia, had had a stroke and entered into a lingering illness. Ever since he had achieved fame in the early Bond films, Connery had been trying to persuade his parents to improve their living conditions at his expense. He had offered to buy them a house in London but they had refused. He had offered to buy them a house in a better part of Edinburgh, and they had accepted only when their tenement flat was under imminent threat of demolition. After his father died of cancer in the seventies, he had tried to persuade his mother to come and join himself and Micheline in Spain. Now, with his mother a semi-invalid, he tried once again but to no avail.

'We're wondering what will be best for her,' he told a reporter on one of the Edinburgh newspapers. 'She prefers to stay here where she can walk around the streets of Edinburgh.' From the start of her illness until her death four years later in 1985, he spent his time shuttling between his home in Spain and, when the restrictions of the Inland Revenue allowed, slipping into Scotland to visit his mother in her bungalow on the southern outskirts of Edinburgh. It was a bad time for him – and as the early eighties passed, Connery stayed holed up in the villa that Micheline had modernized and rebuilt in Marbella, spending time with her, with Jason and stepson Stefan. For once he allowed his professional life in the film industry, which for more than 20 years had dominated his life, to take a back seat.

By now, Jason too was in the acting business and anxious for his father's help and advice. In 1971, when Sean and Diane had split, up he had gone to school at Millfield, a boarding school close to where his mother was living in a commune. He had not been particularly happy there: 'I felt they tried to be too egalitarian and it didn't work. For instance, there was no uniform so you could see who had or didn't have money by their clothes. There were 1,500 pupils and I felt like a number.' He had stayed at Millfield until he was 14 when he asked to leave after a bullied Arab boy hanged himself. He went on to Gordonstoun, a boarding-school in Scotland more famous, perhaps, for its former pupils than its standard of education: Prince Charles, Prince Andrew and Prince Edward all spent time there. Jason was particularly impressed by the level of integration between the school and the local community. 'At Millfield local youngsters think of the pupils as stuck-up snobs. Pupils think of the locals as yobboes. At Gordonstoun that doesn't happen. The school is part of the community.' In his youth Sean Connery himself would have been one of the Millfield 'yobboes' and he was anxious that his son should not grow up a snob.

Accustomed to jet-setting round the world during the holidays, Jason found the school a secure haven. Academically, he did not excel, much to his father's annoyance. 'Dad used to get furious at reports that always read: "Has ability but . . .".'

It was at school that Jason had first become interested in acting. 'Whatever you wanted to do, the school helped you.' He set up a drama club and directed the young Prince Edward in *Hotel Paradiso*. When he decided to leave school before sitting his A levels, a decision which by all accounts did not please his father, acting was his chosen profession. 'Acting as a career seemed too obvious, but as time went by and my interest didn't waver, I knew that that was what I was going to do. I was set to go to the Bristol Old Vic but then auditioned for Perth Rep and decided I'd prefer the practical experience.'

According to Sean, Jason had originally expressed an interest in learning the craft of acting at RADA in London. The self-taught actor in Connery could see the value in stage experience and counselled the young man against formal training.

'At Gordonstoun we saw he obviously wasn't going to do anything academically. When Jason told me he wanted to be an actor and said he wanted to go to RADA, I told him that if he did, it would then be three years before we knew if he could act or not, and I had a different idea. I told him that he'd have to find a job and I suggested he should audition for the theatre. He was accepted for the Bristol Old Vic and for the Perth Repertory. I thought Perth was a better bet because he would learn immediately, and be paid enough to cover his digs. In eight months he had been in two musicals, a pantomime, three plays, had stage managed, got his Equity card and bought a car.'

During his visits to Scotland to visit his ill mother, Connery filmed scenes for a new 35mm documentary at the request of the leader of the local council, to promote the capital as a 'tourist, commercial and conference centre', a film released under the title *Sean Connery's Edinburgh*. Originally asked to do only a voice-over, he became so enthusiastic that he offered to appear in the film as well. The costs were met by the local authority, which put in £50,000, and sponsors Scottish & Newcastle Brewers, the Clydesdale Bank and British Caledonian Airways, each of which put in £10,000. Connery gave his services free of charge, his *quid pro quo* coming in the last scene of the film, after the titles, which was a shot of the brass plaque outside the offices of the Scottish International Education Trust (SIET) with Connery's face reflected in it. Payment was in kind rather than in cash.

Sean Connery's Edinburgh was premièred in Edinburgh on 8 September 1982 and Connery was forthright and unabashed about it: 'It's much better than most films of this kind that I've seen. It's very professional. And witty. I know most of the places we filmed. I'm 52, after all, and I like to think I'm fairly knowledgeable about my home town.'

There was talk at the time about negotiating a distribution deal with Warner Bros but this never came off. 'The problem is that most cinemas run only one major feature and this, at just over half an hour, would be ranked as support,' said Connery. 'But it deserves a wide audience.'

During these four years when he did virtually no filming, Connery was far from idle. He had been nagged for some time by the idea that some of his associates had been swindling him for money and he decided to act. His first target was a former financial adviser, Kenneth Richards who, without his knowledge, had invested a large sum of Connery's money in a French property development company which had gone bankrupt. Richards had already sued him unsuccessfully for money he claimed Connery owed him. Connery, hurt and angry that a man he had trusted had not only let him down but had taken him to court, lodged a suit against Richards for damages and in 1984 was eventually awarded £2.8 million. But Richards, living in Switzerland, was unable to pay and the following year was declared bankrupt, much to Connery's chagrin. 'I have never cheated or stolen from anyone in my life,' Connery was to say later, 'and I'd be quite happy to stick anyone who steals from me in jail.'

Since the sixties Connery had been plagued by feelings that Broccoli and Saltzman had not paid him adequately for his contribution to the creation of the Bond character on screen, and the feelings did not diminish as time wore on. In the years since the launch of *Dr No* in 1962, the hundreds of millions of pounds earned by the films, principally for Broccoli, Saltzman and McClory, contrasted with the sums that Connery, by his own reckoning, had been paid. Spurred by the success of his court action against Richards, Connery mounted a breathtakingly massive claim against Broccoli and United Artists (which had now merged with MGM). The claim, the largest of its kind ever mounted, was for $225 million on the highly technical argument that profit sharing amounted to stock participation. It rumbled on for months and months but was eventually settled out of court. The terms of the settlement were never announced and both parties claimed victory.

*

The Bond films had given Connery the kind of popularity and financial security that, to many actors, is an unattainable dream. Yet they may have had the effect of masking the real talent which Connery had as an actor. It was perhaps for this reason that recognition came late in Connery's career. But come it did, not only from professional bodies in Britain and America but from his home town of Edinburgh.

One of the first bodies to honour him, Heriot-Watt University, awarded him the honorary degree of Doctor of Letters in 1981 'in recognition of the contribution he has made to public entertainment world-wide and to young enterprise in Scotland'. Connery was flattered by the award and planned to attend the ceremony or 'capping' to take place at the university's July graduation ceremony. But in the summer of 1981 he was filming *Five Days One Summer*. Shooting overran its schedule (thus earning Connery overtime) and three days before the ceremony at Heriot-Watt, Connery had to phone the university to postpone his visit. It was rescheduled for the November 'Congregation' at the Assembly Hall in Edinburgh city centre, when he was to be awarded along with other worthies such as Dr Derek Pringle, a nuclear physicist, and Cardinal Gordon Gray, head of the Roman Catholic Church in Scotland. Connery made it here, if only by the skin of his teeth.

'There was a touch of 007 about the eventual graduation day,' according to Donald C. MacDonald, the university's public relations officer. 'Mr Connery had intended taking an early morning scheduled flight from London to Edinburgh to arrive in good time for the Saturday ceremony, but missed this, and the next flight would not reach Edinburgh before the ceremony started. The University, alerted to the problem, decided to start the ceremony as scheduled at 10.30am but sought the co-operation of the police to get Mr Connery from Edinburgh Airport to the Assembly Hall as soon as possible. Bundled into a police car straight off the plane on the tarmac, with motor cycle outriders and sirens blaring, Sean was taken at breakneck speed through the city. Robed, he slipped almost unnoticed into his seat beside Cardinal Gray just as the last of the morning's new graduates were being presented.'

The near-disaster had a lasting effect on university protocol. 'Until that day, those receiving honorary degrees from

Heriot-Watt University had always been the first to be presented . . . at the *start* of the ceremony. Ever since that momentous November morning, honorary graduates have been the last to be presented and have received their degrees at the *end* of the ceremony. Of such is tradition moulded!' says Mr MacDonald.

Heriot-Watt had set a precedent and a couple of years later, on 25 April 1984, Philip Ledger, Principal of the Royal Scottish Academy of Music and Drama in Glasgow, made Connery his personal nomination for the award of a Fellowship in recognition of his 'contribution to the furtherance of education through the Scottish International Education Trust'. Connery wrote back immediately to say that he would be willing to accept the fellowship and 'would wish to attend the ceremony if his schedule allowed him to do so'. In the event it did not and the Fellowship was conferred in July 1984 in his absence.

By 1986 the memories of the problems associated with *Never Say Never Again* had receded. His mother had succumbed to her long illness in 1985 and had been cremated in Mortonhall, a quiet cemetery in her beloved Edinburgh. And his old friend and golfing partner Sir Iain Stewart had committed suicide by shooting himself with a revolver. Gradually Connery began to get back into gear and to become involved once again in films, some, like *The Name of the Rose* and *The Untouchables*, quite outstanding and others, like *Highlander*, quite frivolous.

The Name of the Rose was a collaborative venture between Italy, Germany and France. 'To be poncing around in open-toed sandals and no socks and with a shaved head was no fun at all – it was really freezing,' says Connery, 'but I wasn't worried about playing a celibate after having such a worldly image. At my age, that side of it was easy.'

By the end of August 1986, the week when *The Name of the Rose* came out in the States, Connery was in Chicago filming street scenes for *The Untouchables*, a big-screen version of the television series that had launched Robert Stack into the limelight in the late fifties and early sixties as whiter-than-white cop Eliot Ness. The film was to be directed by Brian De Palma. Just ten days prior to the commencement of filming Sean Connery, cast as wily Irish-American beat cop Jim Malone, was looking forward to working with both De Palma and Bob Hoskins who was to play Al Capone, but Hoskins was dropped at the last minute in favour of Hollywood veteran Robert De Niro.

Although Connery stole the limelight from Costner who played Eliot Ness, he had still not, whether through inability or unwillingness, mastered the American accent well enough to convince even Americans (who, to their credit, are much less accent-conscious than the British). His accent, strongly toned down as it was, had not bothered the North American producers of the Bond films – it was British and that was good enough – but it has perhaps meant that he has never even been considered for some of the great American screen roles, and tends to have had his Scoto-American accent passed off as 'Irish' or he has taken on roles where he plays a foreigner such as in *The Hunt for Red October*. On reviewing *Ransom* (released in the US as *The Terrorists*) *Variety* noted that '. . . at no time does he (Connery) lose his Scottish brogue' and later, in a review of *The Anderson Tapes*, the magazine indicated that 'Essentially miscast but trying mightily to keep his accent under control, Connery's presence is strong.' Some would, however, claim that his accent has matured as it has aged and gained a richness it never had during the Bond era. Connery himself puts it this way: 'Because I'm Scottish I stress certain words differently. I hate the poetry-voice. The poetry should speak for itself. Because of my word-stress I was able to get away from the original Bond character and take the sting out of those bad-taste jokes that crop up in the films.'

Until this point Connery had been honoured only by Scottish academic institutions and, apart from the early Variety Club award for 'creating James Bond' in 1964, his talents as an actor had never been formally recognized by his fellow professionals. When the sun rose over 1988, his performance in *The Untouchables* had already won him the Golden Globe for Best Supporting Actor from the Hollywood Foreign Press Association. And at the beginning of 1988 the British Academy of Film and Television Arts (BAFTA) not only short-listed him as Best Supporting Actor for that film, but also as Best Actor for *The Name of the Rose*. *The Untouchables* was a success both at the box-office and with the critics and it received a clutch of Oscar nominations. For the first time in his career, Connery received a nomination, as Best Supporting Actor.

Thirty years after taking his first faltering steps in the film industry, he arrived in Hollywood for the Oscars to a warm welcome. He was one of the Grand Old Men of the films. He had been around for a long time and he was well liked for his honesty, his humility, his directness. And it was to be *his* night. In the face of competition from Albert Brooks (*Broadcast News*), Morgan Freeman (*Street Smart*), Denzel Washington (*Cry Freedom*) and Vincent Gardenia (*Moonstruck*) he won his first and, to date, his only, Oscar. 'I first appeared here 30 years ago,' he said as he accepted the award, referring presumably to his time in Hollywood when filming *Darby O'Gill and the Little People.* 'Patience is a virtue.'

Michael Caine was more forthcoming: 'That was a great moment for him. You'd never get him to say it, but I'll bet you it was one of the greatest things to happen to him. It shook him to the core.'

The Oscar nomination and the award itself were perhaps not all that surprising in themselves, but something that happened during the ceremony certainly was. 'When he came out to get his Oscar,' says Caine, 'he got a standing ovation from the cream of Hollywood.' He had been given a standing ovation for a Best Supporting Actor Oscar. 'I'll bet you nobody's ever done that,' says Caine.

Only a few months after the Oscar, he was to receive another award, this time from the University of St Andrews. Connery had been a frequent visitor to the home of golf ever since his love of the sport had been engendered during the filming of *Goldfinger* in 1964 and since, a few years later, Sir Iain Stewart nominated him for membership of the Royal and Ancient. It was not until 8 July 1988, however, that he received an honorary Doctor of Literature degree from the university. He received the award in person and combined his visit with a golfing holiday. Just before he left the ceremony, he was asked by a local reporter if he was going to defend his title as holder of the Queen Victoria Jubilee Vase he had won the previous year in St Andrews. 'Actually, I'm just off to the golf course after this to get some more practice,' came the reply.

Full recognition of his talents by the British film industry

145

came two years later on 7 October 1990 at a ceremony in the Odeon, Leicester Square, when he received the BAFTA-Shell Tribute award for 'his outstanding contribution to world cinema'. The award had been instituted in 1988 and Connery was only its third recipient, the previous two having been Dirk Bogarde and Julie Andrews. His friends in the industry from both sides of the Atlantic turned up to see him accept the award – Harrison Ford, Roger Moore, Michael Caine, Ursula Andress, Gina Lollobrigida and more – and to hear the Princess Royal say: 'He's a professional about everything and works very hard – and that is not only on the screen. The things he has done for young people off screen in this country are tremendous. Maybe we are short of real heroes, but he is a shining example of a hero for a whole generation.'

Connery's voice shook with emotion as he accepted the award. 'I certainly didn't expect anything like this,' he said. 'For someone who never knows what his response is going to be to a situation like this it is very difficult to prepare and I am caught out again.'

For Michael Caine, the award ceremony showed what Connery had missed by 'locking himself away' in Marbella between 1981 and 1985, 'a place where he doesn't even speak the language.

'I think he has suffered. He had been quite isolated in Marbella and he thought nobody cared. When the BAFTA award came, there were all these people who had come just to honour him. He suddenly realized that all these people really did care about him.'

In his emotionally charged acceptance speech, Connery told the audience: 'I've had a 30-year film odyssey and met some really marvellous people. But what became apparent this evening was that I have not seen them as much as I should have.' Or, as he told Caine afterwards: 'I don't know why I've locked myself away in Marbella. It's so much fun with everybody here.'

Why was success so long in coming? Partly, no doubt, because the frivolity of the Bond films gave people the impression that he was a frivolous actor. Partly, perhaps, because his refusal totally to submerge his Scottish accent has restricted the scope and variety of the parts he has been offered. And partly because he has accepted too many parts in bad films. He has admitted himself that he has had more than his fair share of abject failures.

One factor may be that he has never quite outgrown his boyhood passion for adventure stories. Perhaps this is one reason for his appearance in *Highlander*, shot in London, Scotland and New York, and released in 1985. The Highlander, Connor McLeod of the Clan McLeod, played by Christopher Lambert, is one of a breed of what are apparently superhumans. He survives an apparently fatal stabbing by the Black Knight, another superhuman, and encounters Juan Sanchez Villa Lobos of Ramirez, played by Sean Connery (yet another superhuman), an Egyptian with a Scottish accent and a Spanish name, who is later to be killed by the Black Knight.

In 1989 Connery co-starred in another adventure movie, *Indiana Jones and the Last Crusade*, directed by Steven Spielberg. This fairy tale starred Harrison Ford as Indiana Jones, a young archaeologist in 1938 on the track of the legendary Holy Grail. Connery, at his brilliant bantering best, plays Professor Henry Jones.

In 1990, *The Hunt for Red October* was released. Connery, looking his most distinguished, plays Rameus, the commander of a new class of Soviet nuclear submarine. The film has all the ingredients of excitement and tension but the technicalities of the plot make it difficult to follow in places. Also, there is no female interest and the cast is almost entirely male. Nevertheless, *Variety* wrote that: 'Sean Connery is splendid as the renegade Soviet nuclear sub captain pursued by . . . the fleets of both superpowers'.

By now, films were virtually guaranteed a modicum of success with Connery's name above the title and were being put together entirely around his participation. *The Russia House*, also released in 1990 and based on John Le Carré's novel of the same name, would never have been made without Connery in the starring role. Here he plays a Scottish London-based publisher with a fondness for whisky, being manipulated into a love affair by MI6. The five-week filming schedule in Leningrad and Moscow was arranged entirely to suit him.

Highlander II – The Quickening, another 1990 release, was a curious follow-up to the original. Although Connery had been beheaded in *Highlander*,he comes back to life in *Highlander II*. He reappears on the stage of a play being shown in Glencoe, Scotland and travels to Edinburgh to be kitted out as a Highland gent before becoming involved in the nitty-gritty of the story. Though his part is small and of no relevance to the overall plot, he plays the part to perfection and with consummate humour.

In the same year that *Highlander II – The Quickening* was being shot, Connery was filming yet another Sidney Lumet film, *Family Business*, in New York. He was about to fly out to Canada to do a part he had signed up for in the film version of the Tom Stoppard play *Rosencrantz and Guildenstern Are Dead*, which was being directed on screen by Stoppard himself, when something happened which caused him much consternation. He thought he had cancer. During the filming of *Family Business* he developed a sore throat. 'I had what sounded like laryngitis,' he said.

Ever since he was a young naval rating, Connery had been known for his apparent fear of hospitals. 'He's a terrible hypochondriac,' says Michael Caine. 'He always seems to have something wrong with him. It's all imaginary.'

According to Jason Connery, his father also has a fear of needles. 'We both went to have a full medical for insurance,' he said. And when the doctor produced a needle to take a blood sample, 'Dad almost passed out. He gets a bit queasy when he thinks about that kind of stuff.'

But this throat condition was different and Connery steeled himself and went to see a specialist. 'He scared the hell out of me by saying "Well, I've never seen anything like this before".'

Fortunately, Connery had a non-malignant condition similar to the throat polyps which singers are prone to, and after taking several other opinions, he decided to do as he was being advised and rest his voice for a month prior to being operated upon, talking to no-one for that period of time.

Filming of *Rosencrantz and Guildenstern Are Dead* was due to start just a few days later and Connery contacted Tom Stoppard to tell him he could not do it. The whole project had been financed and set up around Connery – Canada had been chosen as the location, for example, because Connery was unable to work in the United States or in the UK for tax reasons. When Connery told him about his throat problem, Stoppard wanted to wait until he was better but Connery refused on the basis that he did not know how long that would take.

According to Connery, Stoppard then sent round the 'heavies'. 'I had given my word that I was going to do it. Then they came round with a lawyer. They thought I was on some dodge – I've since had four operations. I couldn't have gone into court on it. And eventually I gave him £300,000 to get out of it. Normally I would have sued Stoppard out of the country. He . . . was privy to what the whole thing was about. He behaved very badly.'

The idea of his home town honouring Sean Connery had been mooted in Edinburgh as early as 1966. At that time a proposal to organize a civic lunch for him was put before the Lord Provost's Committee but was withdrawn before a vote could be taken. It was not until years later that a civic lunch was, in fact, organized to coincide with the charity gala showing of *Diamonds Are Forever* in Edinburgh in 1972. This may have had more to do with his setting up of the Scottish International Education Trust, however, than with Connery's achievements as an actor.

But the crowning glory for Connery was initiated on 16 November 1990 when Councillor Eleanor McLaughlin, Lord Provost of Edinburgh, tabled a motion to the General Purposes Committee 'That the Freedom of the City be conferred on Sean Connery to celebrate his distinguished contribution to world cinema; to mark his largely unpublicized work in founding the Scottish International Education Trust whose aims include the promotion of individual Scottish talent; and in particular to recognize the respect and high esteem in which he is held by the people of the City of Edinburgh.' Eleanor McLaughlin had already approached Connery and he had told her he would be delighted to accept. Coincidentally, the motion was seconded by Irene Kitson, daughter of Alex Kitson, Connery's old workmate at the St Cuthbert's dairy in Fountainbridge.

When the idea of giving him the Freedom of the City was first proposed, there was some opposition to the idea. A few prominent local worthies objected on the basis that such an important honour should not be awarded to an Edinburgh man who had abandoned his native land because he was unwilling to pay the taxes. When the vote was taken in the council chamber on 20 December 1990 on whether to sanction the award, a two-thirds majority was needed to approve it. In the event 49 voted to make the award, eight against – two Labour and six Conservative. As one of those who voted against, Councillor Gerry Coutts, put it: 'I had no hesitation in paying tribute to his outstanding film career but the honour should have been given to someone for more important reasons. There are many people who are far more deserving of the award.' Much was made of the fact that Prince Charles, the Prince of Wales, had been proposed for the award in the 1970s – and had been turned down!

But the people of Edinburgh were massively in favour. The local evening newspaper, the *Evening News*, ran a phone-in on the subject and more than 90 per cent of callers were in favour of it.

When Connery was approached to see whether he would accept such an award, he was enthusiastic. 'When I was first approached about it I didn't really understand the historical significance of it,' he said. The Freedom of the City is the top honour Edinburgh can bestow on anyone and an award which had been in existence since 1459. It has been given in the past to writers such as Scott, Johnson, Smollett and Dickens, to politicians such as Disraeli, Lloyd George and Winston Churchill, to explorers such as Livingstone and Stanley, and to scientists such as Sir James Young Simpson and Alexander Graham Bell. 'I think I'm the first from Fountainbridge,' said Connery.

Not only had the Freedom of Edinburgh never been awarded to someone from the Fountainbridge area before, it had never before been awarded to a film actor, the closest, perhaps, having been Sir Harry Lauder, 'entertainer', in November 1927. When Connery was nominated there were only five other living freemen, including Queen Elizabeth, Prince Phillip, and the virtuoso violinist Yehudi Menuhin. According to the local press, there were six others. Connery, they said, was to be the seventh – or, as the headline writers had it the following day, the '007th'.

Connery flew into Edinburgh on 10 June 1991 straight from filming *Medicine Man* in the jungles of Mexico where he was playing Dr Robert Campbell, a Scottish (we are left to presume) field researcher who has been working from a hideaway in the rain forest and believes he has found a cure for cancer.

The event took place on 11 June 1991 amid a welter of publicity. The day began with a press conference, at which he had some rather harsh words to say about the *Scotsman*. The newspaper had printed an article by Brian Prendreigh on the morning of the award which was somewhat less than complimentary about Connery. Prendreigh had been desperately trying to get an individual interview with Connery, to no avail.

'Now he is a reclusive multi-millionaire with homes in Spain, California and The Bahamas,' wrote Prendreigh. 'Connery has long been canny with the bawbees [halfpennies], demanding $1 million to play Bond for a sixth time in *Diamonds Are Forever*.

'Connery recently split £250,000 between the [Scottish International Education] trust and Dundee, St Andrews and Heriot-Watt University. The American film magazine *Premiere* reported that he recently received $500,000 for one day's work in the cameo role of King Richard in *Robin Hood, Prince of Thieves*. [Jim] Houston confirmed that the recent donation came from *Robin Hood* money. *Variety* calculated Connery's total earnings at $35 million last year.

'He has chosen to live abroad and every time he steps ashore in Britain, the taxman's clock starts ticking towards that elusive point where he can claim a share of the millions.'

Connery read the *Scotsman* article over breakfast in the Balmoral Hotel and as the morning wore on, became increasingly annoyed, not so much at what the article had explicitly stated but about the implications of what the journalist had written.

In his opening remarks to the journalists assembled at the press conference, Connery said: 'There are a couple of things that got up my nose this morning in the *Scotsman*. This chap [Prendreigh] wanted to know how much I gave to charity. To give you an example of how difficult the answer is, there's a film called *Robin Hood, Prince of Thieves*.' Kevin Costner, he went on, had asked him to play a day in the film as King Richard – 'It's only half a page.' Connery agreed to do it for a fee of £250,000 on the condition that he could give the money to charity, and it was split equally between the Scottish International Education Trust, Heriot-Watt University, St Andrews University and Dundee Cancer. 'The way it read it was as though one was getting $250,000 and professing to give it to charity.

'Another inference was that I don't pay taxes, which is entirely untrue. When I moved out of Britain in 1974 I paid nothing but taxes on everything that was frozen in the country. You're not allowed to take money out. And I pay full tax in Britain and America whenever I work, with none of the benefits of living in the country.'

He finished with typical acerbity: 'You can ask any question you want and I'll decide whether it's your business or not.'

The press conference was followed by a visit to the Canaan Project, a home for the elderly blind, on behalf of which Connery accepted two cheques totalling £18,500 from the Braid Committee and from the Edinburgh Solicitors Property Centre. He also presented a bouquet to local broadcaster Mary Marquis in appreciation of her work for the charity. Finally, at 6.30pm it was off to the Usher Hall for the award itself.

When he had been offered the award, Connery had insisted that he wanted 'the ordinary folk' of Edinburgh to receive priority when tickets were distributed for the Usher Hall ceremony. The organizers had agreed and were later to report that the response was such that they could have filled the hall five times over. Consequently, when Connery arrived that evening, the hall was packed to capacity. A crowd of well-wishers, who had been unable to get tickets, waited outside for the Great Man to arrive. When his limousine, provided by the local council, drew up, he shook hands, talked briefly with the people in the crowd and then stepped inside. It was a triumphal home-coming for Connery and the people turned out in force to greet him.

The Freedom of the City award involves presenting the recipient at a ceremony with a 'burgess ticket' which is traditionally handed over in a silver casket. In Connery's case, the constraints of local government expenditure meant that he was presented with his burgess ticket in a casket made from American black walnut with silver mounts.

The presentation ceremony was presided over by Tom

Conti, another Edinburgh man, music being provided by Mike Hart and his jazz band. The film *Sean Connery's Edinburgh* was shown as well as a video montage of his commercial films. Finally, there were speeches by Conti, Eleanor McLaughlin and Connery.

When Connery stood up to speak, a male voice from the audience set the tone of the evening. 'Welcome home Big Tam,' he shouted. Big Tam was touched. He could make no reply.

'The Freedom of Edinburgh has a marvellous ring to it and I'm more than proud to accept such a great honour,' he said in his acceptance speech. 'When I was first informed about the possibility of receiving the Freedom of Edinburgh, I knew that I would not be able to express my thanks adequately in words. I *can* tell you how I feel. I feel like I've gone 15 rounds with Mike Tyson – but I won!'

7

THE NATIONALIST

7

The Nationalist

I'm what I always have been – a Scot, a bit introspective. I don't tell lies and I prefer straight dealing.

Sean Connery

If those Labour and Conservative councillors who had voted in favour of giving Connery the Freedom of the City of Edinburgh in 1990 had known that just nine months later he was to make public his support for the Scottish Nationalists in the most dramatic way, there might have been more than just eight who baulked at the idea of giving him the award.

In many ways Connery was born to be a socialist and his friends from the fifties and sixties understood him to be a tacit, if inactive, supporter of the Labour Party. He was from dyed-in-the-wool working-class stock. He was born in an area of traditional solid Labour support. But Connery's nationalist leanings can be traced right back to his time in the Royal Navy, his first foray outside his native Scotland. Here he met and mixed with English naval recruits, doubtless subjected to the ribald comments about Scottish meanness and accent mimicry. The jesting must have hit home and he had his right arm tattooed with the words 'Scotland Forever'.

But in the sixties and seventies a variety of events caused him to transfer his allegiance from the socialists to the nationalists. One was the surge of popular support which occurred in the mid-sixties for the Scottish National Party (SNP) due largely to the discovery of substantial oil fields off the Scottish coast. This led to the election of a clutch of

Members of Parliament. Another factor in Connery's conversion was his involvement in the Fairfields Experiment, also in the mid-sixties, and the making of the television documentary *The Bowler and the Bunnet*. This project, which for Connery was more important than all of the Bond films put together, and which to date is his only venture into the world of directing films, made him realize that he had links with Scotland that no amount of separation would ever break. Yet another factor was his disillusionment with the Labour Party which had cold-bloodedly brought the Fairfields Experiment to a premature end by merging it into Upper Clyde Shipbuilders.

It had been way back in 1967, while making *The Bowler and the Bunnet*, that he had first showed his hand in a letter to George Leslie who was fighting a by-election for the nationalists in Glasgow. In the letter he spoke of building a 'self-governing Scotland' in which the Scottish people could take pride and which would take its place among the community of nations. At the beginning of 1969 he took the more dramatic step of allowing it to be made known that his name was on a short-list of prospective Scottish National Party candidates for the West Fife constituency, a seat held by Labour MP Willie Hamilton with a 17,000 majority in the 1966 election.

Almost before the news was out, it was being denied by SNP leaders. According to a report in the *Scotsman* on 9 January 1969: 'News that the West Fife constituency of the Scottish National Party want to invite Sean Connery . . . to become a prospective Parliamentary candidate was greeted with surprise by party leaders last night.'

Rather embarrassingly, his name had to be withdrawn when it was discovered that it had not been cleared by the relevant SNP committee and that in any case he was not even a member of the party.

Later in the year he was quoted in a Scottish Sunday newspaper as saying: 'Everywhere I travel in the world I keep bumping into Scotsmen. It seems to me all wrong that so much talent should be leaving the country. So along with several top Scottish businessmen I hope to have an investigation into this drain to see if there is anything which can be done to stop it.' It was partly as a result of this investigation that he, Sir Iain

Stewart and Jim Houston set up the Scottish International Education Trust (SIET).

In September 1991, just a few months after Connery had received the Freedom of Edinburgh, reports began to appear in the press that he was to make his most public statement of support so far for the Scottish National Party. His messages of support for the party were to be the spearhead of a new publicity campaign and he was to do a voice-over for a party political broadcast. The script for the five minute broadcast talked of Scotland becoming an independent nation within the European Community and, according to a party spokesman, Connery was 'more than happy to argue that it is absolutely ridiculous to be spending money on nuclear weapons rather than on the health service.' Press publicity around the time of the broadcast claimed that the party had gained at least 1,000 new members as a result; Connery was, however, publicly criticized by a group of 14 Scottish MPs for his decision to do the voice-over and also for appearing in an advertisement for Japanese whisky.

He was quick to reply. 'I have a birthright in Scotland,' Connery told a television reporter. 'I have supported Scotland with my work because I pay taxes, with none of the benefits. If I had chosen the field of government, I would have chosen to govern my country, which is Scotland. I don't think I would have gone to London to govern Scotland.'

Worse was to follow. In April 1992, prior to the cinema release of *Medicine Man*, he was interviewed by a journalist from the Australian *Woman's Weekly* magazine which had dug out the comments he had made when he was much younger about violence towards women. These comments had been picked up by *Playboy* in 1965 ('An openhanded slap is justified if all other alternatives fail and there has been plenty of warning') and this in turn had been picked up by Barbara Walters who had interviewed him for American television in 1991. Earlier on, in 1986, he had reiterated his feelings in *Woman* magazine. When journalist Duncan Fallowell mentioned the original 1961 interview with Susan Barnes, Connery told him: 'I still go along with that.'

In the *Woman's Weekly* article Connery claimed that his original comments 30 years previously had been taken out of context. 'I actually said there is something worse than striking a woman. It is demoralizing her, demeaning her. The same with a man. I said that that is worse than smacking her.

'There are so many causes. A guy lives in a tenement, has three children, works all day, and he's got a problem with his wife. He doesn't have a club to go to. He can't walk out, and if she wants some kind of confrontation, it's very difficult for it not to materialize.'

Previously his remarks had not caused much consternation, but in 1992 a general election was imminent and he had publicly declared his support for the Scottish Nationalists. Questions were raised in the House of Commons and the next day the *Scotsman* reported that '26 MPs had signed a Commons motion saying they were appalled by the remark by Mr Connery.

'Margaret Ewing, parliamentary leader of the SNP, said . . . that the remarks had been taken out of context.

'Mrs Ewing claimed the story came from an interview with Mr Connery on a television chat show in the United States 31 years ago and the actor had made no such statement in it.

'The Labour MPs, led by Maria Fyfe (Glasgow, Maryhill), had urged the SNP to dissociate itself from the remark, saying they were "appalled at the views expressed by Connery in an Australian magazine that giving a woman a smack in the face is acceptable conduct and that she is 'looking for' such behaviour on the part of her partner or husband".

'Mrs Ewing, MP for Moray, said yesterday that the original interview took place in 1961. "In it, Connery spelled out the unacceptability of violence towards women and also drew attention to the many, varied and tortuous ways in which women can be demeaned."'

The story was taken up a few days later by *Sunday Times* journalist Anne Smith. 'Last week in *Woman's Weekly*, an Australian magazine, Sean Connery explained: "Demoralizing a woman, demeaning her, is much worse than striking her."

'No doubt the actor was led into making this remark . . . but at 61 he is old enough to have learned more sense.

'Far from coming across as a sage man in the autumn of his days, Connery is beginning to sound as if his emotional development had stopped round about his 17th birthday . . .'

Even when he had made the voice-over for the SNP party political broadcast, Connery was still not a member of the party. He had been giving it his tacit support for more than two decades but he had never joined. This was to come later and was to be instigated by Gordon Wright, an Edinburgh-based publisher of Scottish and Scottish nationalist books. Years previously, after reading an interview in *Scotland on Sunday* in which Connery had expressed his support for the Scottish Nationalist cause, Wright had sent Connery a copy of the recently published *Scotland: A Concise History*, written from a nationalist viewpoint by an ex-chairman of the Scottish National Party. In 1981, he sent Connery another book, this time a copy of *Tales of Sir William Wallace* with the suggestion (never taken up) that it be made into a film. After a couple of subsequent telephone conversations with Connery, Wright asked him why he had never joined the SNP. 'No-one ever asked me,' came the reply.

As a result, it was Gordon Wright who finally signed Connery up as a card-carrying member of the SNP on 31 January 1992. The membership, which was processed through the Newington branch of the SNP on the south side of Edinburgh, took even the party headquarters by surprise. By pure coincidence his membership card carried the number '007'.

Connery's 'Scottishness' has several times threatened to extend in a more positive way into his professional life. In addition to his work on a film script for *Macbeth* way back in the sixties, he has also toyed with the idea of turning one of Scottish writer William McIlvanney's novels into a film. When *Laidlaw* was published in 1977 he telephoned McIlvanney in Kilmarnock and arranged a clandestine meeting in the tea-room at Edinburgh Zoo. He told McIlvanney that he wanted to direct the film and play the lead and that McIlvanney would write the script. In turn, he asked McIlvanney if he would hold off selling the film rights for the book until he, Connery, had made efforts to raise the money in America. McIlvanney agreed to this, but a year later he had heard nothing more and fresh interest in the film rights to *Laidlaw* was emanating from North America. He wrote to Connery telling him he was planning to option the film rights elsewhere and, after receiving a letter from Connery wishing him well, he optioned the film rights to Jay Julian in New York.

Connery's public irritation with the trappings of fame came to the fore once again during this meeting. McIlvanney became aware of one of the serving women constantly looking across at the pair. Eventually, she approached the table and said to Connery: 'Are you who I think you are?'

'No,' said the Great Man bluntly, and the woman retreated.

The simple and effective ways Connery has developed for dealing with fame conceal a more complex character beneath. 'He has a disarming core of shyness,' says McIlvanney. 'And for a man who has achieved what he has achieved, it's very endearing. It's as if he's strong enough to be vulnerable.'

To McIlvanney, Connery represents much of what is best in the Scottish male tradition. 'He's very much his own man,' he says. 'He knows who he is and there's no phoniness. Yes, he's changed a lot, but only according to his personal modification of the principles he was brought up to believe in when he was in Fountainbridge. I think that's the way to do it.

'He has parameters he lives within and borders you don't cross. He's got a sense that you don't invade his space. It's not an aggression – it's an answer to aggression. He's a very benign and psychologically generous person – but don't trample on his toes.'

For McIlvanney, one of the keys to the Scottish character, and to Connery's inner being, has been the lack of materialism in a country which has never been prosperous. 'He obviously likes money,' he says of Connery, 'but there's also a sense of a man who has human values. He's not a bad representative of a pretty hard and sometimes brutalizing tradition. When he enters a room he walks in his own collateral. He's survived wealth without succumbing to using it as a measurement of himself. Not too many rich or powerful people can do that. Their status blurs their sense of themselves. But I get the feeling that if Sean lost every penny tomorrow he'd still be a man of substance. He'd still know who he is.'

Sean Connery's abilities as a screen actor have been neatly summed up by director Steven Spielberg in an interview following the successful release of *Indiana Jones and the Last Crusade* in 1989. By virtue partly of his presence and charisma on the screen and partly of his sheer professionalism as an actor, Connery 'stole' the show and produced a performance as memorable, at least, as that of Harrison Ford.

'Sean wasn't supposed to be introduced until page 70 of the script, but he kept coming up with so many extra scenes that we put him in 20 pages earlier. Then we added more scenes with him later. He was instrumental in all the rewrites. When he gets a good idea, which is about 20 times a day, he's such a child. His face lights up.

'He's from the old school. The complete professional. He has to say his lines wordperfect. There was one scene in which he was supposed to say something like "I knew I had to get that book as far away from me as possible" and he kept messing up one word. He would insist that we do it again. We did it seven times. It became such a joke on the set that we were going to have teeshirts made up with the line on them.

'Sean Connery is not like anybody else. He's an original. He's never been stronger or more sought after and he's finally recognized as the movie star he's always been. Sean is one of the great movie stars. He'll be remembered throughout history.'

And some years later, John McTiernan, who directed Connery in *Medicine Man*, made further fulsome comments: 'It's almost like he's some extraordinary modelling clay. He can become different people and each one is archetypically large and each one can be very different. No matter what circumstances you put him in, a rigid and intimidating ship's captain or an old reprobate working in the rain forest in tattered clothes and old sneakers, there's always something riveting about him.'

FILMOGRAPHY/IMPORTANT DATES

Filmography/Important Dates

This section combines significant dates with a concise filmo-
graphy which together summarize Connery's career.
Film dates are those of first release in the UK, television dates
are those of first transmission, while theatre dates are those of
first public performance. Other dates are self-explanatory.

1930
25 August. Euphamia Connery gives birth to a son Thomas in
the Royal Maternity Hospital, Edinburgh.

1935
August. Tommy Connery goes to his first school, Tollcross
Primary in Fountainbridge.

1937
Tommy Connery is moved to Bruntsfield Primary School for
the remainder of his primary education.

1939
Tommy Connery takes job delivering milk in the mornings
before going to school.

1942
August. Tommy Connery goes to Darroch School.

1944
June. Tommy Connery finishes at Darroch School and starts working full-time as a milk-delivery man at the St Cuthbert's Dairy, Fountainbridge.

1947
Tommy Connery joins the Royal Navy for seven years (and five in the Naval Reserve), initially as a boy sailor, and travels south to Portsmouth barracks.

1949
Tommy Connery is discharged from naval service with a small pension. Retrains as a French polisher.

1952
December. The Glorious Days at the Edinburgh Empire Theatre starring Anna Neagle. Connery plays the part of a court usher.

1953
June. Joins cast of *South Pacific* at the Theatre Royal, Drury Lane, London and then goes on tour round the UK. Connery starts off in the chorus and progresses through the cast during the run, eventually having a small speaking part.

1955
8 November. Witness for the Prosecution at the Q Theatre, West London. Director: Robert Henderson. Script: Agatha Christie. Cast: Mary Cambridge, Bill Davies, Neil Wilson, Peter Lindsay, Ronald Wood, Phillip Holles, Violet Loxley, Vernon Smythe, Robert White, Sean Connery, Henry Rayner, John Healey, Frederick Keen, Audrey O'Flynn, Rosemary Wallace.
22 November. Point of Departure at the Q Theatre. Director: Frederick Farley. Script: Jean Anouilh (translated by Kitty Black). Cast: Meadows White, Ian Bannen, Edna Hazell, Vernon Smythe, Martin Wyldeck, Dorothy Grumbar, Lucy Garde, Ivor Dean, Philip Olles, Jennifer Wright, Irene Richmond,

Robert Sansom, Sean Connery, Ronald Sowton, John Healey.
20 December. A Witch in Time at the Q Theatre. Director: Robert Henderson. Script: Dolph Norman. Cast: Ellen Pollock, Susan Richards, Beatrice Rowe, Shirley Cooklin, Sean Connery, Audrey O'Flynn, Terence O'Regan, Michael Partridge.

1957
18 February. No Road Back, UK. Director: Montgomery Tully. Producer: Steve Pallas. Screenplay: Charles A. Leeds and Montgomery Tully. Distributor: RKO Radio. Cast: Skip Homeier, Paul Carpenter, Margaret Rawlings, Sean Connery.
31 March. BBC: *Requiem for a Heavyweight.* Director: Alvin Rakoff. Cast including Sean Connery, Jacqueline Hill, Warren Mitchell.
19 August. Time Lock, UK. Director: Gerald Thomas. Producer and screenplay (from a play by Arthur Hailey): Peter Rogers. Distributor: British Lion. Cast: Robert Beatty, Betty McDowall, Vincent Winter, Lee Patterson, Alan Gifford, Robert Ayres, Victor Wood, Jack Cunningham, Peter Mannering, David Williams, Larry Cross, Gordon Tanner, John Paul, Donald Ewer, Murray Kash, Sean Connery.
August. ATV Playhouse: *Anna Christie.*
20 August. Hell Drivers, UK. Director: Cy Endfield. Producer: Benjamin Fisz. Screenplay: John Kruse and Cy Endfield. Distributor: Rank. Cast: Stanley Baker, Patrick McGoohan, Herbert Lom, Peggy Cummins, William Hartnell, Wilfred Lawson, Jill Ireland, Sidney James, Gordon Jackson, Sean Connery.
23 September. Action of the Tiger, UK. Director: Terence Young. Producer: Kenneth Harper. Screenplay (based on a novel by James Wellard): Robert Carson. Distributor: MGM. Cast: Van Johnson, Martine Carl, Herbert Lom, Gustavo Rocco, Anthony Dawson, Helen Haye, Sean Connery.

1958
2 June. Another Time, Another Place, US. Director: Lewis Allen. Producer: Lewis Allen and Smedley Aston. Screenplay (from a novel by Lenore Coffee): Stanley Mann. Distributor: Paramount. Cast: Lana Turner, Barry Sullivan, Glynis Johns, Sean Connery, Sidney James.

1959

5 May. The Bacchae at Oxford Playhouse. Company: The Meadow Players. Director: Minos Volanakis. Script: Euripides (translated by Minos Volanakis). Cast: Michael David, David Dodimead, Edward Hardwicke, Sean Connery, Charles Laurence, Christopher Hancock, Yvonne Mitchell.

21 June. Tarzan's Greatest Adventure, UK. Director: John Guillernin. Producer: Sy Weintraub. Screenplay: Lawrence Edward Watkin. Distributor: Paramount. Cast: Gordon Scott, Anthony Quayle, Sara Shane, Niall MacGinnis, Sean Connery, Scilla Gabel.

27 July. Darby O'Gill and the Little People, US. Director: Robert Stevenson. Producer/Distributor: Walt Disney, US. Screenplay (from the 'Darby O'Gill' books by H. T. Kavanagh): Lawrence Edward Watkin. Cast: Albert Sharpe, Sean Connery, Jimmy O'Dea, Janet Munro, Kieron Moore, Estelle Winwood, Walter Fitzgerald, Denis O'Dea, J. G. Devlin, Jack MacGowran.

12 October. The Sea Shell at the Royal Lyceum, Edinburgh. Script: Jess Gregg. Cast: Sybil Thorndike, Heather Sears, Sean Connery.

3 November. ATV: *The Crucible* by Arthur Miller. Producer: Henry Kaplan. Cast: Barbara Chilcott, Susannah York, Sean Connery, Noel Willman.

1960

17 January. BBC: *Colombe* by Anouilh. Producer: Naomi Capon. Cast: Françoise Rosay, Dorothy Tutin, Freda Jackson, Sean Connery, Patrick Wymark, Peter Sallis.

29 March. Anna Christie at the Oxford Playhouse. Company: the Meadow Players. Director: Douglas Seale. Script: Eugene O'Neill. Cast: Gordon Pitt, Glenn Beck, Christopher Smith, Redmond Phillips, Wauna Paul, Jill Bennett, Chris Cherry, Sean Connery, David Buxton.

12 May. BBC: *Richard II* in 'Age of Kings' series. Plays Hotspur. Producer: Peter Dews. Director: Michael Hayes. Cast including David William, Tom Fleming, Sean Connery.

26 May. BBC: *Henry IV* in 'Age of Kings' series. Plays Hotspur. Producer: Peter Dews. Director: Michael Hayes. Cast including Frank Pettingel, Robert Hardy, Tom Fleming, Sean Connery.

28 September. BBC: *Riders to the Sea*. Script: J. B. Synge. Cast:

Sybil Thorndike, Olive McFarland, Jan Kenny, Sean Connery.

11 October. ITV: *The Pets* (adaptation of the novel *The Hiding Place* by Robert Shaw). Director: Peter Wood. Cast: Max Adrian, Robert Shaw, Sean Connery.

4 November. Naked at the Oxford Playhouse. Director: Minos Volanakis. Company: the Meadow Players. Script: Luigi Pirandello (translated by Simon Nedia). Cast: Diane Cilento, Frank Thornton, Phyllis Montefiore, David Jackson, Sean Kelly, Rosamund Waring, Sean Connery.

1961

12 June. BBC: *Adventure Story.* Plays Alexander the Great. Script: Terence Rattigan. Producer: Randolph Cartier.

September. The Frightened City, UK. Director: John Lemont. Producers: John Lemont and Leice Nance. Distributor: Anglo-Amalgamated. Cast: Herbert Lom, John Gregson, Yvonne Romaine, Sean Connery.

29 October. On the Fiddle, UK. (US: *Operation SNAFU*). Director: Cyril Frankel. Producer: Benjamin Fisz. Screenplay: Harold Buchman. Distributor: Anglo-Amalgamated. Cast: Alfred Lynch, Sean Connery, Cecil Parker, Stanley Holloway, Alan King, Eric Barker, Wilfrid Hyde White, Kathleen Harrison, Eleanor Summerfield, Terence Longdon, Victor Maddern, Harry Locke, John Le Mesurier, Edna Morris.

3 November. BBC: *Anna Karenina.* Plays Vronsky. Cast including Claire Bloom, Sean Connery, Albert Lieven.

1962

8 October. Dr No, UK. Director: Terence Young. Producers: Albert R. Broccoli and Harry Saltzman for Eon Productions Ltd. Script (from novel by Ian Fleming): Richard Maibaum, Johanna Harwood and Berkely Mather. Distributor: United Artists. Cast: Sean Connery, Ursula Andress, Joseph Wiseman, Jack Lord, Bernard Lee, Anthony Dawson, John Kitzmiller, Zena Marshall, Eunice Gayson, Lois Maxwell, Peter Burton.

12 October. The Longest Day, US. Producer/Director: Darryl F. Zanuck. Screenplay (based on his own book of the same name): Cornelius Ryan. Distributor: Twentieth Century-Fox. Cast: John Wayne, Robert Mitchum, Henry Fonda, Robert Ryan, Richard Todd, Richard Burton, Kenneth More, Peter Lawford,

Leo Genn, John Gregson, Sean Connery, Jack Hedley, Michael
Medwin, Norman Rossington, Paul Anka, Robert Wagner.
29 November. Marries Diane Cilento at Registry Office on Gibraltar.

1963
11 January. Jason Connery is born in Rome.
27 October. From Russia with Love, UK. Director: Terence Young.
Producers: Albert R. Broccoli and Harry Saltzman for Eon Pro-
ductions Ltd. Screenplay: Richard Maibaum adapted by
Johanna Harwood. Distributor: United Artists. Cast: Sean Con-
nery, Daniella Bianchi, Pedro Armendariz, Lotte Lenya, Robert
Shaw, Bernard Lee, Eunice Gayson, Walter Gotell, Nadja Rgin,
Lois Maxwell, Aliza Gur, Martine Beswick, Valdek Sheybal,
Desmond Llewellyn.

1964
August. Woman of Straw, UK. Director: Basil Dearden. Producer:
Michael Relph. Screenplay (based on a book by Catherine
Arley): Robert Muller, Stanley Mann and Michael Relph. Dis-
tributor: United Artists/Novus. Cast: Gina Lollobrigida, Sean
Connery, Ralph Richardson, Johnny Sekka, Laurence Hardy,
Danny Daniels, A. J. Brown, Peter Madden, Alexander Knox,
Edward Underdown, George Curzon, Andre Morell, Robert
Bruce, Peggy Marshall.
August. Marnie, US. Director: Alfred Hitchcock. Producer:
Alfred Hitchcock. Screenplay (based on a book by Winston
Graham): Jay Presson Allen. Distributor: Universal. Cast: Sean
Connery, Tippi Hedren, Diane Baker, Martin Gabel, Louise
Latham, Bob Sweeney, Alan Napier, S. John Launer, Mariette
Hartley, Bruce Dern, Henry Beckman, Meg Wylie.
17 September. Goldfinger, UK. Director: Guy Hamilton. Pro-
ducers: Albert R. Broccoli and Harry Saltzman for Eon Produc-
tions Ltd. Screenplay: Richard Maibaum and Paul Dehn.
Distributor: United Artists. Cast: Sean Connery, Honor Black-
man, Gert Frobe, Shirley Eaton, Tania Mallet, Harold Sakata,
Bernard Lee, Cec Linder, Lois Maxwell, Desmond Llewellyn.

1965
June. The Hill, UK. Director: Sidney Lumet. Producer: Kenneth

Hyman. Screenplay (based on an autobiographical play, *Breaking Point* by Ray Rigby): Frank R. Cunningham. Distributor: MGM. Cast: Harry Andrews, Sean Connery, Ian Hendry, Alfred Lynch, Jock McGrath, Roy Kinnear, Norman Bird, Ian Bannen.

16 December. Thunderball, UK. Director: Terence Young. Producer: Kevin McClory for Eon Productions Ltd. Executive Producers: Albert R. Broccoli and Harry Saltzman. Screenplay (based on an original story by Kevin McClory, Jack Whittingham and Ian Fleming): Richard Maibaum and John Hopkins. Distributor: United Artists. Cast: Sean Connery, Claudine Auger, Adolfo Celi, Luciana Paluzzi, Rik Van Nutter, Bernard Lee, Martine Beswick, Guy Doleman, Lois Maxwell, Desmond Llewellyn.

1966

14 February. Scottish Television: *Fairfields – Keel of Industry,* documentary in 'Present Grandeur' series. Sean Connery speaks commentary.

July. Announces retirement from Bond role while filming *You Only Live Twice* in Japan.

September. A Fine Madness, US. Director: Irvin Kershner. Producer: Jerome Hellman. Screenplay (based on his own book of the same name): Elliott Baker. Distributor: Warner-Pathé. Cast: Sean Connery, Joanne Woodward, Jean Seberg, Patrick O'Neal, Colleen Dewhurst, Clive Revill, Werner Peters, John Fiedler, Kay Medford, Jackie Coogan, Zohra Lampert, Sue Ann Langdon, Sorrell Booke, Bibi Osterwald, Mabel Albertson.

1967

31 January. Volpone at the Garrick Theatre, London. Director: Frank Hauser. Presented by Peter Bridge in association with Sean Connery.

13 March. The Diary of a Madman at the Duchess Theatre, London. A one-man play by Walter Eysselink, adapted from the story by Nikolai Gogol. Director: Irvin Kershner. Presented by Peter Bridge in association with Sean Connery. Cast: Nicol Williamson.

12 June. You Only Live Twice, UK. Director: Lewis Gilbert. Producers: Albert R. Broccoli and Harry Saltzman for Eon

Productions Ltd. Screenplay: Roald Dahl. Distributor: United Artists. Cast: Sean Connery, Akiko Wakabayashi, Tetsuro Tamba, Mie Hama, Teru Shimada, Karin Dor, Donald Pleasence, Bernard Lee, Lois Maxwell, Desmond Llewellyn, Charles Gray.

18 July. Scottish Television: *The Bowler and the Bunnet.* Director: Sean Connery. Producer: Bryan Izzard for Sean Connery and Scottish Television. Screenplay: Cliff Hanley.

The Molly Maguires, US. Director: Martin Ritt. Producers: Martin Ritt and Walter Bernstein. Screenplay: Walter Bernstein. Distributor: Paramount. Cast: Richard Harris, Sean Connery, Samantha Eggar, Frank Finlay, Anthony Zerbe, Bethel Leslie.

1968

September. Shalako, UK. Director: Edward Dmytryk. Producer: Euan Lloyd. Screenplay (based on a book by Louis L'Amour): J. J. Griffith, Hal Hopper and Scott Finch. Distributor: Kingston. Cast: Sean Connery, Brigitte Bardot, Peter Van Eyck, Stephen Boyd, Honor Blackman, Jack Hawkins, Woody Strode, Eric Sykes, Alexander Knox, Valerie French, Julian Mateos, Donald Barry, Rodd Redwing, Elmer Smith, Hans De Vries, Walter Brown, Charles Stainaker, Bob Cunningham, John Clark, Bob Hall.

1969

La Tenda Rossa, Italy/USSR. (UK: *The Red Tent*). Director: Mikhail Kalatozov. Producer: Franco Cristaldi. Screenplay: Ennio de Concini and Richard Adams. Distributor: Paramount. Cast: Sean Connery, Claudia Cardinale, Hardy Kruger, Peter Finch, Massimo Girotti, Luigi Vanucchi.

1 February. ATV: *MacNeil.* Connery plays title role.

16 December. I've Seen You Cut Lemons at the Fortune Theatre, London. Director: Sean Connery. Presented by Geve Persson in association with Sam Coslow. Script: Ted Allen. Cast: Diane Cilento, Robert Hardy.

1970

13 March. Meets Micheline Roquebrune at international golf tournament in Casablanca.

4 & 5 July. Sean Connery Pro-Am Golf Tournament at Troon, Scotland.

4 December. Inauguration of Scottish International Education Trust.

1971

8 October. The Anderson Tapes, US. Director: Sidney Lumet. Producer: Robert M. Weitman. Screenplay (based on a book by Lawrence Sanders): Frank R. Pierson. Distributor: Columbia. Cast: Sean Connery, Dyan Cannon, Martin Balsam, Alan King, Ralph Meeker, Christopher Walken.

30 December. Diamonds Are Forever, UK. Director: Guy Hamilton. Producers: Albert R. Broccoli and Harry Saltzman for Eon Productions Ltd. Screenplay (based on a novel by Ian Fleming): Richard Maibaum and Tom Mankiewicz. Distributor: United Artists. Cast: Sean Connery, Jill St John, Charles Gray, Lana Wood, Jimmy Dean, Bruce Cabot, Bernard Lee, Lois Maxwell, Putter Smith, Bruce Glover, Marc Lawrence, Desmond Llewellyn.

1973

March. The Offence, UK. Director: Sidney Lumet. Producer: Denis O'Dell. Screenplay (based on his own stage play *This Story of Yours*): John Hopkins. Distributor: United Artists. Cast: Sean Connery, Trevor Howard, Vivien Merchant, Ian Bannen, Derek Newark, Peter Bowles.

4 October. Obtains divorce decree from Diane Cilento because the couple had lived apart for two years.

1974

Zardoz, UK. Director/Producer/Screenplay: John Boorman. Distributor: Twentieth Century-Fox. Cast: Sean Connery, Charlotte Rampling, Sara Kestelman, John Alderton, Sally Ann Newton, Niall Buggy.

Ransom, UK (US: *The Terrorists*). Director: Casper Wrede. Producer: Peter Rawley. Screenplay: Paul Wheeler. Distributor: MGM. Cast: Sean Connery, Ian McShane, Norman Bristow, John Cording, Isabel Dean, William Fox.

Murder on the Orient Express, UK. Director: Sidney Lumet. Producers: John Bradbourne and Richard Goodwin. Screenplay:

Paul Dehn. Distributor: EMI. Cast: Albert Finney, Ingrid Bergman, Lauren Bacall, Martin Balsam, Jacqueline Bisset, Jean-Pierre Cassel, Sean Connery, John Gielgud, Wendy Hiller, Anthony Perkins, Vannessa Redgrave, Rachel Roberts, Richard Widmark, Michael York, Colin Blakely, George Coulouris, Denis Quilley, Vernon Dubtcheff, Jeremy Lloyd, John Moffatt.

1975

6 May. Marries Micheline Boglio Roquebrune on Gibraltar.
26 October. The Wind and the Lion, US. Director/Screenplay: John Milius. Producer: Herb Jaffe. Distributor: Columbia-Warner. Cast: Sean Connery, Candice Bergen, Brian Keith, John Huston, Geoffrey Lewis, Steve Kanaly, Roy Jensen, Vladek Sheybal, Darrel Fetty, Nadim Sawalha, Mark Zuber, Anthoine St John, Simon Harrison, Polly Gottesman, Deborah Baxter, Luis Bar Boo, Akio Miamura.

1976

18 April. The Man Who Would Be King, US. Director: John Huston. Producer: John Foreman. Screenplay (from a story by Rudyard Kipling): John Huston and Gladys Hill. Distributor: Allied Artists. Cast: Sean Connery, Michael Caine, Christopher Plummer, Saeed Jaffrey, Karroum Ben Bouih, Jack May, Dughmi Larbi, Shakira Caine, Mohammed Shamsi, Paul Antrim, Albert Moses, Kimal Singh, Gurmuks Singh, Yvonne Ocampo, Nadia Atbib.
The Next Man, US. Director: Richard C. Sarafian. Producer: Martin Bregman. Screenplay: Mort Fine, Alan R. Trustman, David M. Wolf and Richard C. Sarafian. Distributor: Harris Films. Cast: Sean Connery, Cornelia Sharpe, Adolfo Celi, Marco St John, Ted Beniades, Charles Cioffi.
Robin and Marian, US. Director: Richard Lester. Producer: Denis O'Dell. Screenplay: James Goldman. Distributor: Columbia-Warner. Cast: Sean Connery, Audrey Hepburn, Robert Shaw, Richard Harris, Nicol Williamson, Denholm Elliott, Kenneth Haig, Ronnie Barker, Ian Holm, Bill Maynard, Esmond Knight, Veronica Quilligan, Peter Butterworth, John Barrett, Kenneth Cranham, Victoria Merida Roja, Montserrat Julio, Victora Hernandez Sanguino, Mararita Mingullion.

1977

A Bridge Too Far, US. Director: Richard Attenborough. Producer: Joseph E. Levine. Screenplay (from Cornelius Ryan's book of the same title): William Goldman. Distributor: United Artists. Cast: Dirk Bogarde, James Caan, Michael Caine, Sean Connery, Edward Fox, Elliott Gould, Gene Hackman, Anthony Hopkins, Hardy Kruger, Laurence Olivier, Ryan O'Neal, Robert Redford, Maximilian Schell, Liv Ullmann.

1978

The First Great Train Robbery, UK. Director/Screenplay: Michael Crichton. Producer: John Foreman. Distributor: United Artists. Cast: Sean Connery, Donald Sutherland, Lesley-Anne Down, Alan Webb, Malcolm Terris, Robert Lang, Wayne Sleep, Michael Elphick, Pamela Salem, Gabrielle Lloyd, James Cassins, John Bett, Peter Benson, Janine Duvitski, Agnes Bernelle, Frank McDonald, Brian De Salvo, Joe Cahill, Pat Layde, Derek Lloyd, Rachel Borrows.

1979

Meteor, US. Director: Ronald Neame. Producers: Sandy Howard and Gabriel Katzka. Screenplay (from story by Edmund H. North): Stanley Mann and Edmund H. North. Distributor: Palladium. Cast: Sean Connery, Natalie Wood, Karl Malden, Brian Keith, Martin Landau, Trevor Howard, Richard Dysart, Henry Fonda, Joseph Campanella, Bo Brundin, Roger Robinson, James Richardson, Katherine De Hetre, Michael Zaslov, Gregory Gay, Bibi Besch, John Findlater.

Cuba, US. Director: Richard Lester. Producers: Arlene Sellers and Alex Winitsky. Screenplay: Charles Wood. Distributor: United Artists. Cast: Sean Connery, Brooke Adams, Jack Weston, Hector Elizondo, Denholm Elliott, Martin Balsam.

1981

14 November. Receives honorary degree of Doctor of Letters from Heriot-Watt University.

Outland, UK. Director/Screenplay: Peter Hyams. Producer: Richard A. Roth. Distributor: Columbia-EMI-Warner. Cast: Sean Connery, Peter Boyle, Francis Sternhagen, James B. Sikking, Kika Markham.

Time Bandits, UK. Director/Producer: Terry Gilliam. Screenplay: Michael Palin and Terry Gilliam. Distributor: Handmade Films. Cast: John Cleese, Sean Connery, Shelley Duvall, Katherine Helmond, Ian Holm, Michael Palin, Ralph Richardson, Peter Vaughan, David Warner, David Rappaport, Craig Warnock.

1982

The Man with the Deadly Lens, UK (US: *Wrong Is Right*). Director/Producer/Screenplay (based on a book by Charles McCarry): Richard Brooks. Distributor: Columbia. Cast: Sean Connery, George Grizzard, Robert Conrad, Katharine Ross, G. D. Spradlin, John Saxon.

Five Days One Summer, US. Director/Producer: Fred Zinnemann. Screenplay (based on Kay Boyle's short story, *Maiden, Maiden*): Michael Austin. Distributor: Warner. Cast: Sean Connery, Betsy Brantley, Lambert Wilson, Jennifer Hilary, Isabel Dean, Gerard Buhr.

8 September. Sean Connery's Edinburgh. Director: Murray Gregor. Producers: Lynda Myles and Murray Gregor. Narrator: Sean Connery.

1983

Never Say Never Again, US. Director: Irvin Kershner. Producer: Jack Schwartzman. Screenplay: Lorenzo Semple Jr, based on *Thunderball*, by Kevin McClory, Jack Whittingham and Ian Fleming. Distributor: Columbia. Cast: Sean Connery, Klaus Maria Brandauer, Max Von Sydow, Barbara Carrera, Kim Basinger, Alex McCowen, Edward Fox.

Sword of the Valiant – The Legend of Gawain and the Green Knight. Director: Stephen Weeks. Screenplay: Stephen Weeks, Philip M. Breen, Howard C. Pen. Distributor: Cannon. Cast: Miles O'Keeffe, Trevor Howard, Sean Connery, Peter Cushing, Ronald Lacey, Cyrielle Claire, Emma Sutton, Douglas Wilmer, Lila Kedrova.

1984

25 April. Royal Scottish Academy of Music and Drama decides to award Fellowship to Sean Connery.

1985

Sean Connery's mother dies after a lingering illness.

Sir Iain Stewart commits suicide.

Highlander, US. Director: Russell Mulcahy. Producers: Peter S. Davis and William N. Panzer. Screenplay: Gregory Widden, Peter Bellwood and Larry Ferguson. Distributor: EMI. Cast: Christopher Lambert, Roxanne Hart, Clancy Brown, Sean Connery, Beatie Eney, Alan North, Sheila Gish.

The Name of the Rose, Italy/Germany/France. Director: Jean-Jacques Annaud. Producer: Bernd Eichinger. Screenplay (based on a book by Umberto Eco): Andrew Birkin, Gerard Brach, Howard Franklin and Alain Godard. Distributor: Twentieth Century-Fox. Cast: Sean Connery, Christian Slater, Helmut Qualtinger, Elya Baskin, Michael Lonsdale, Volker Preschtel, Feodor Chaliapin Jnr, William Hickey, Michael Habeck, Urs Althaus, Valentina Vargas.

1987

2 March. Awarded *Commandeur des Arts et des Lettres* by French Ministry of Foreign Affairs.

The Untouchables, US. Director: Brian De Palma. Producer: Art Linson. Screenplay: David Mamet. Distributor: Paramount. Cast: Kevin Costner, Sean Connery, Charles Martin Smith, Andy Garcia, Robert De Niro, Richard Bradford.

1988

11 April. Receives Oscar as Best Supporting Actor for his performance in *The Untouchables*.

8 July. Awarded honorary DLitt by University of St Andrews.

The Presidio, US. Director: Peter Hyams. Producer: D. Constantine Conte. Screenplay: Fred Caruso. Distributor: UIP. Cast: Sean Connery, Mark Harmon, Meg Ryan, Jack Warden, Mark Blum, Dana Gladstone.

1989

Indiana Jones and the Last Crusade, US. Director: Steven Spielberg. Producer: Robert Watts. Screenplay: Jeffrey Boam. Distributor: UIP. Cast: Harrison Ford, Sean Connery, Denholm Elliott, Alison Doody, John Rhys-Davies, Julian Glover, River Phoenix, Michael Byrne, Kevork Malikyan, Robert Eddison,

Richard Young, Alexei Sayle.

Family Business, US. Director: Sidney Lumet. Producer: Lawrence Gordon. Screenplay (based on his own book): Vincent Patrick. Distributor: Palace. Cast: Sean Connery, Dustin Hoffman, Matthew Broderick, Rosana DeSoto, Janet Carroll, Victoria Jackson, Bill McCutcheon, Deborah Rush, B. D. Wong.

1990

The Hunt for Red October, US. Director: John McTiernan. Producer: Mace Neufeld. Screenplay (based on a book by Tom Clancy): Larry Ferguson and Donald Stewart. Distributor: Paramount. Cast: Sean Connery, Alec Baldwin, Scott Glenn, Sam Neill, James Earl Jones, Joss Ackland.

The Russia House, US. Director: Fred Schepisi. Producers: Brian Maslansky and Fred Schepisi. Screenplay (based on a novel by John Le Carré): Tom Stoppard. Distributor: UIP. Cast: Sean Connery, Michelle Pfeiffer, Roy Scheider, James Fox, James Mahoney, Michael J. Kitchen, J. T. Walsh, Ken Russell, David Threlfall, Klaus Maria Brandauer.

7 October. BAFTA makes annual Tribute award to Sean Connery for outstanding contribution to world cinema.

Highlander II – The Quickening, US. Director: Russell Mulcahy. Producers: Peter S. Davis and William Panzer. Screenplay: Peter Bellwood. Distributor: EMI. Cast: Christopher Lambert, Sean Connery, Virginia Madsen, Michael Ironside, Alan Rich, John C. McGinley.

20 December. Edinburgh District Council decides to honour Sean Connery with the Freedom of Edinburgh.

1991

Robin Hood, Prince of Thieves, US. Director: Kevin Reynold. Producers: John Watson, Pen Densham and Richard B. Lewis. Screenplay: Pen Densham and John Watson. Distributor: Warner. Cast: Kevin Costner, Morgan Freeman, Mary Elizabeth Mastrantonio, Christian Slater, Alan Rickman, Sean Connery, Geraldine McEwan, Michael McShane, Brian Blessed, Michael Wincott, Nick Brimble.

11 June. Presented with the Freedom of the City of Edinburgh.

1992

27 January. Awarded *Chevalier de la Légion d'Honneur* by French Ministry of Foreign Affairs.

31 January. Joins Scottish National Party.

29 May. Medicine Man, US. Director John McTiernan. Producers: Andrew G. Vajna and Donna Dubrow. Executive Producer: Sean Connery. Screenplay: Tom Schulman and Sally Robinson. Distributor: Guild. Cast: Sean Connery, Lorraine Bracco, Jose Wilker, Rodolfo de Alexandre.

BIBLIOGRAPHY

Bibliography

Bardot, a Personal Biography by Glenys Roberts. Sidgwick & Jackson, 1984

Bardot, an Intimate Biography by Willi Frischauer. Michael Joseph, 1978

Best of Times, Worst of Times by Shelley Winters. Frederick Muller, 1990

Detour: A Hollywood Tragedy – My Life with Lana Turner, my Mother by Cheryl Crane with Cliff Jahr. Michael Joseph, 1988

Diana Dors' A–Z of Men by Diana Dors. Futura, 1984

From Limelight to Satellite: A Scottish Film Book edited by Eddie Dick. BFI Publishing/Scottish Film Council, 1990

Hitchcock, the Definitive Study by François Truffaut. Martin Secker & Warburg, 1968

Hybrid by Diane Cilento. Hodder & Stoughton, 1970

Knock Knock by Candice Bergen. Hamish Hamilton, 1984

Lana the Lady, the Legend, the Truth by Lana Turner. New English Library, 1982

Michael Caine by Philip Jodge. Spellmount, 1985

On Q by Kenneth Barrow. De Leon Memorial Fund in association with Heritage Publications, 1992

Richard Harris: Actor by Accident by Gus Smith. Robert Hale, 1990

Room at the Top: Golf the Bob Torrance Way by Bob Torrance with

Norman Mair; foreword by Sean Connery. Mainstream, 1988
Scratch an Actor by Sheilah Graham. W. H. Allen, 1969
Sean Connery, a Biography by Kenneth Passingham. Sidgwick &
Jackson, 1983
Sidney Lumet: Film and Literary Vision by Frank R. Cunningham.
University Press of Kentucky, 1991
Sybil Thorndike Casson by Elizabeth Sprigge. Victor Gollancz,
1971
The Life of Ian Fleming by John Pearson. Jonathan Cape, 1966
The Manipulator by Diane Cilento. Hodder & Stoughton, 1968
There's Always Tomorrow, an Autobiography by Anna Neagle. W.
H. Allen, 1978
Whatever Happened at Fairfields? by Bill Hawkins and Sydney
Paulden. Gower Press, 1969
What's It All About by Michael Caine. Century, 1992
Within Whicker's World by Alan Whicker. Elm Tree, 1982
You Only Live Once by Ivar Bryce. Weidenfeld & Nicholson,
1984

Index